D0122159

Straight Shooting

STRAIGHT SHOOTING

FIREARMS, ECONOMICS AND PUBLIC POLICY

JOHN R. LOTT, JR.

Merril Press
Bellevue, WA 98005

Straight Shooting

is published by

Merril Press, P.O. Box 1682, Bellevue, WA 98009.

Web: www.merrilpress.com

Phone: 425-454-7009

Distributed to the book trade by

Midpoint Trade Books, 27 W. 20th Street, New York, N.Y. 10011

Web: www.midpointtradebooks.com

Phone: 212-727-0190

FIRST EDITION

LIBRARY OF CONGRESS CATALOGING-IN-PUBLICATION DATA

Straight shooting: guns, economics, and public policy / by John R.
Lott. --1st ed.
  p.cm.
ISBN 0-936783-47-8
1. Gun control --United States. 2. United States --Economic Conditions
-- 2001- 3. United States--Politics and government --2001- I.Title.

HV7436.L685 2⁰⁰⁶   **60969763**
363.3'3'0973 --(

PRINTED IN THE UNITED STATES OF AMERICA

To Armen A. Alchian,
who helped teach me how
to apply economics to
everyday problems.

PART ONE

Guns, Safety, and the Second Amendment

The Big Lie of the Assault Weapons Ban: The Death of the Law Hasn't Brought a Rise in Crime—Just the Opposite • Canada Blames Us: Gun-Control Folly Here, Up North, Across the Pond... • Watch-List "Justice" • Weapons Bans Miss the Mark • Right-to-Carry Law is the Way to Go • *60 Minutes*, Terrorists and Guns • Good Samaritan Gun Use • Banning Guns in the U.K. Has Backfired • Gunning for Cheney • How Can Anyone Oppose Letting Retired Police Carry Guns? • Time to Level Playing Field for Gun Makers • Gun Control Remains a Loaded Issue for Democratic Candidates: The Rhetoric May be Toned Down, but the Aim Remains the Same • Athletes and Guns • P.C. Air Security: When Will Our Pilots Be Armed? • Half Cocked: Why Most of What You See in the Media About Guns is Wrong. • The Ban Against Public Safety: D.C. Gun Laws Have Increased Crime • Right to Carry Would Disprove Horror Stories • United Nations vs. Guns: An International Gun-Control Fight • Armed, and Safer, Iraqis • Bad Sports: A Church Turns Down $10,000 from Sportsmen • Scare Tactics on Guns and Terror • When Gun Laws Don't Make Sense • Bullets and Bunkum: The Futility of "Ballistic Fingerprinting" • Democrats Have Not Dropped Gun Control Agenda • Shooting Blanks • When It Comes to Firearms, Do as I Say, Not as I Do: Rosie O'Donnell, Who Opposes Handgun Permits for Others, Doesn't See a Problem with Her Bodyguards Having Them • "The Patriot" is Right • The Cold, Hard Facts About Gun • Rampage Killing Facts and Fantasies • Will Questioning Our Neighbors Make Us Safer? • Armed Response to Shooting Didn't Really Make the News • Gun Control Misfires in Europe

PART TWO

Other Freedoms, Studies and Musings

Bogus Discrimination Claims • Affirmative Action Has Mixed Results for Cops • An Organization Pregnant with Contradictions • Unserious Suggestions: Silly Democratic Consultations • High on Hype: Congress "Takes On" Steroids • The Felon Vote • Social Security Reform Won't Boost U.S. Debt • Eliminating Sentencing Guidelines Would Make Penalties More Equal • Exploding the Fireworks Safety 'Threat' • Moore's Myths • Sampling of Entire State Refutes Selective Error-Data • Voting Machine Conspiracy Theories • Let the Market Work Even During Disasters • Statistical Mishmash Muddles Unemployment Rates • Does Release Of Terror Info Do More Harm Than Good? • Supreme Irrelevance: Will the high Court be Undone by Political Reality? • Baghdad's Murder Rate Irresponsibly Distorted • Let the Sunshine In • Rush, by the Numbers? • Divorcing Voters, Again: Supreme-Court Campaign-Finance Reform Case Gets Heard • The Drug World's Easy Riders • When Welfare is Disguised as a Tax Cut • Unequal Punishment • Much Ado About Nothing • States May Regret Reforms • Records of Retiring Politicians Defy Campaign-Reform Logic • Don't Mess with Texas • Partisan Bias in Newspapers? A Study of Headlines Says Yes

PART ONE

Guns, Safety,
and the Second Amendment

The Big Lie of the Assault Weapons Ban:
The Death of the Law Hasn't Brought a Rise in
Crime—Just the Opposite

This wasn't supposed to happen. When the federal assault weapons ban ended on September 13, 2004, gun crimes and police killings were predicted to surge. Instead, they have declined.

For a decade, the ban was a cornerstone of the gun control movement. Sarah Brady, one of the nation's leading gun control advocates, warned that "our streets are going to be filled with AK-47s and Uzis." Life without the ban would mean rampant murder and bloodshed.

Well, more than nine months have passed and the first crime numbers are in. Last week, the FBI announced that the number of murders nationwide fell by 3.6% last year, the first drop since 1999. The trend was consistent; murders kept on declining after the assault weapons ban ended.

Even more interesting, the seven states that have their own assault weapons bans saw a smaller drop in murders than the 43 states without such laws, suggesting that doing away with the ban actually reduced crime. (States with bans averaged a 2.4% decline in murders; in three states with bans, the number of murders rose. States without bans saw murders fall by more than 4%.)

And the drop was not just limited to murder. Overall, violent crime also declined last year, according to the FBI, and the complete statistics carry another surprise for gun control advocates. Guns are used in murder and robbery more frequently then in rapes and aggravated assaults, but after the assault weapons ban ended, the number of murders and robberies fell more than the number of rapes and aggravated assaults.

It's instructive to remember just how passionately the media hyped the dangers of "sunsetting" the ban. Associated Press headlines warned "Gun shops and police officers brace for end of assault weapons ban." It was even part of the presidential campaign: "Kerry blasts lapse of assault weapons ban." An Internet search turned up more than 560 news stories in the first two weeks of September that expressed fear about ending the ban. Yet the news that murder and other violent crime declined last year produced just one very brief paragraph in an insider political newsletter, the Hotline.

The fact that the end of the assault weapons ban didn't create a crime wave should not have surprised anyone. After all, there is not a single published academic study showing that these bans have reduced any type of violent crime.

Research funded by the Justice Department under the Clinton administration concluded only that the effect of the assault weapons ban on gun violence "has been uncertain." The authors of that report released their updated findings last August, looking at crime data from 1982 through 2000 (which covered the first six years of the federal law). The latest version stated: "We cannot clearly credit the ban with any of the nation's recent drop in gun violence."

Such a finding was only logical. Though the words "assault weapons" conjure up rapid-fire military machine guns, in fact the weapons outlawed by the ban function the same as any semiautomatic—and legal—hunting rifle. They fire the same bullets at the same speed and produce the same damage. They are simply regular deer rifles that look on the outside like AK-47s.

For gun control advocates, even a meaningless ban counts. These are the same folks who have never been bashful about scare tactics, predicting doom and gloom when they don't get what they want. They hysterically claimed that blood would flow in the streets after states passed right-to-carry laws letting citizens carry concealed handguns, but that never occurred. Thirty-seven states now have right-to-carry laws—and no one is seriously talking about rescinding them or citing statistics about the laws causing crime.

Gun controllers' fears that the end of the assault weapons ban would mean the sky would fall were simply not true. How much longer can the media take such hysteria seriously when it is so at odds with the facts?

Originally appeared June 28, 2005 in the Los Angeles Times.

Canada Blames Us:
Gun-Control Folly Here,
Up North, Across the Pond...

If you have a problem, try blaming it on someone else. And with Canada's murder rate rising 12% last year and the recent rash of murders by gangs this year in Toronto and other cities, it is understandable that Canadian politicians want to blame someone else. That at least was the strategy by Canada's Premiers when they met last Thursday with the new U.S. Ambassador to Canada, David Wilkins, and spent much of the meeting blaming their problems on guns being smuggled from the United States.

Of course, there is a minor little problem with the attacks on the U.S.. Canadians really don't know what the facts are. The reason is simple: despite billions of dollars spent on Canada's gun registration program and the program not actually solving any crimes, the government does not even know the number of crime guns seized in Canada, let alone where those crime guns came from. The Royal Canadian Mounted Police reported in late July that they "cannot know if [the guns] were traceable or where they might have been traced." Thus, even if smuggled guns were an important problem, the Canadian government doesn't know if it is worse now than in the past.

Even in Toronto, which keeps some track of these numbers, Paul Culver, a senior Toronto Crown Attorney, claims that guns from the U.S. are a "small part" of the problem.

There is another more serious difficulty: you don't have to live next to the United States to see how hard it is to stop criminals from getting guns. The easy part is getting law-abiding citizens to disarm. The hard part is getting the guns from criminals. The drug gangs that are firing guns in places such as Toronto seem to have no trouble getting the drugs that they sell and it should not be any more surprising that they can get the weapons they need to defend their valuable property.

The experiences in the U.K. and Australia, two island nations whose borders are much easier to monitor, should also give Canadian gun controllers some pause. The British government banned handguns in 1997 but recently reported that gun crime in England and Wales nearly doubled in the four years from 1998/1999 to 2002/2003.

Crime was not supposed to rise after handguns were banned. Yet since 1996, the serious violent crime rate has soared by 69%; robbery is up by 45% and murder is up by 54%. Before the law, armed robberies had fallen by 50% from 1993 to 1997, but as soon as handguns were banned the robbery rate shot back up—almost to their 1993 levels.

The 2000 International Crime Victimization Survey, the last survey done, shows the violent-crime rate in England and Wales was twice the rate in the U.S. When the new survey for 2004 comes out later this year, that gap will undoubtedly have widened even further as crimes reported to British police have since soared by 35%, while declining 6% in the U.S.

Australia has also seen its violent crime rates soar to rates similar to Britain's immediately after its 1996 Port Arthur gun control measures. Violent crime rates averaged 32% higher in the six years after the law was passed (from 1997 to 2002) than they did the year before the law in 1995. The same comparisons for armed robbery rates showed increases of 74%.

During the 1990s, just as Britain and Australia were more severely regulating guns, the U.S. was greatly liberalizing individuals' abilities to carry guns. Thirty-seven of the 50 states now have so-called right-to-carry laws that let law-abiding adults carry concealed handguns once they pass a criminal background check and pay a fee. Only half the states require some training, usually around three to five hours' worth. Yet crime has fallen even faster in these states than the national average. Overall, the states in the U.S. that have experienced the fastest growth rates in gun ownership during the 1990s have experienced the biggest drops in murder rates and other violent crimes.

Many things affect crime; the rise of drug-gang violence in Canada as well as Britain is an important part of the story, just as it has long been important in explaining the U.S.'s rates. (Few Canadians appreciate that 70% of American murders take place in just 3.5% of our counties and what a large percentage of those murders are drug gang related.) Drug gangs can't simply call up the police when another gang encroaches on their turf, so they end up essentially setting up their own armies. And just as they can smuggle drugs into the country, they can smuggle in weapons to defend their turf.

With Canada's violent crime rate about twice the U.S.'s according to the *International Crime Victimization Survey*, Canada's politicians are understandably nervous.

While it is always easier to blame another for your problems, the solution to crime is often homegrown.

Originally appeared August 19, 2005 in the National Review Online.

Watch-List "Justice"

with Sonya D. Jones

Should people lose rights because they are sympathetic to, but do not actually help, terrorist groups? Should law enforcement and not judges be the arbiter of those sympathizers who should be placed on "watch lists"?

In Senate hearings on renewing the Patriot Act last week, Democratic Senators Ted Kennedy and Charles Schumer said the answer to both questions was "yes." Attorney General Alberto Gonzales and FBI Director Robert Mueller were grilled over a report showing that 35 gun purchases during the first half of last year were made by people on terrorist "watch lists," and the Senators called it a major public security risk.

Messrs. Kennedy and Schumer's proposed solution? Simply ban the sale of guns to people law enforcement places on the watch list.

The *New York Times* also sounded the alarm last week with an editorial entitled, "An Insecure Nation." The *Times* could not resist further sensationalizing the concerns. Fanning fears of terrorists being "free to buy an AK-47," it failed to mention that in the worst case these would be civilian, semi-automatic versions of the guns (just like any hunting rifle), not the machine guns used by militaries around the world.

The 35 "suspect" purchases, out of 3.1 million total transactions, were allowed because background checks found no prohibiting information. No felonies or disqualifying misdemeanors, for example. They were neither fugitives from justice nor illegal aliens. Nor had they ever disavowed their U.S. citizenship.

As Mr. Mueller pointed out, the FBI was alerted when these sales took place, but the transactions weren't stopped because the law didn't prohibit them. But Mr. Mueller assured the Senators that "we then will pursue [these leads]. We will not let it go."

Ironically, this debate occurred just weeks after the U.S. Supreme Court rejected state laws that use police reports to set prison sentences because police reports are not reliable. Being on the "watch list" would also just rely on police reports. There would be no adjudication by a judge, no trial by jury, before being placed on the list. "Suspects" don't even have to be foreigners. They may have simply been individuals classified by law enforcement as sympathetic to militia groups or other "undesirable" domestic organizations.

Some politicians have recently experienced being on a "watch list" firsthand.

Interestingly, the same Senator Kennedy who wants to rely on "watch lists" was understandably upset last year and publicly complained to the Senate Judiciary committee when he was prevented from flying on an airplane because his name was placed on just such a "watch list." Rules did not allow him to be told at the airport why he was being denied a ticket, but fortunately for him, being a U.S. senator meant the problem was eventually resolved with a few telephone calls.

Ultimately, though, despite all the fears generated, background checks simply aren't the solution. The federal Brady Act has been in effect for 11 years and state background checks even longer. But despite all the academic research that has been done, a recent National Academy of Sciences report could not find any evidence—not a single published academic study—that background checks reduce any type of violent crime.

Surely, it would be nice if these regulations worked. But it's hard to believe they will be any more successful stopping terrorists than they have been at stopping criminals. Criminals and terrorists share much in common, starting with the fact that what they are doing is illegal. In addition, terrorists are probably smarter and engage in vastly more planning than your typical criminal, thus making the rules even less likely to be successful.

People need to remind themselves that a "watch list" is only that. It is not even probable cause. If you had probable cause that these suspects had done something illegal, you could arrest them.

Ironically, during the hearing, Mr. Kennedy spent most of his question time concerned that foreign combatants held in Guantanamo were not treated by the military with the respect that the FBI uses to handle American criminals. At the same time, he believes Americans can lose their rights to own a gun without an evidentiary hearing.

Democrats may think that people on "watch lists" should be denied their rights to own a gun, but what is next? Why not just make the system much "more efficient" and simply put all people on "watch lists" directly in prison?

Originally appeared April 11, 2005 in the Washington Times.

Weapons Bans Miss the Mark

Australians are a dangerous lot. Weapons that would hardly cause a second thought in the hands of a citizen in another country generate concern when held by an Australian.

Fortunately, some Australian state governments have understood the dangers of letting ordinary Australians get access to weapons such as laser pointers, a popular device for making business and academic presentations in countries such as the United States.

Americans may feel safe when an academic addresses a conference using a laser pointer. In the hands of an Australian, however, there is understandable fear that these devices could do untold harm. An Australian academic with a laser pointer would cause real panic.

Now the Victorian Government is achieving international recognition for protecting Australians from a danger that has been around for far too long: swords. After July 1, swords will be banned and violators will face penalties that previously have been reserved for laser pointers—six months in jail and a $12,000 fine.

Swords are broadly defined as a cutting or thrusting weapon with a long blade, a hilt and one or two sharp edges. Although this unfortunately exempts knives with either no sharp or three or more sharp edges, or knives without handles, not specifying a blade length in the legislation hopefully ensures many knives will be banned.

A licensing process will be set up so that a select few will be granted an exemption for a $135 fee, but they will have to lock their weapons in sturdy safes and put in burglar alarms. If properly enforced, the law could produce other benefits, such as ensuring that dishes are promptly washed after dinner so that any offending steak knives can be placed back in their safe.

On the downside, the knives would still be available during dinner when many family arguments might get out of hand. It is also not clear if the family will be able to use the knives if the license holder is not present.

And if Australians can't be trusted with laser pointers or swords, they surely can't be trusted with guns. Citizens in other countries are obviously much more trustworthy. Americans, for example, can own all these items. Indeed, 46 states in the U.S. even trust millions of law-abiding Americans to carry concealed handguns when walking on the street or eating in restaurants.

And, yes, in most states an academic addressing a conference or a class can carry a gun and a laser pointer. Over the decades, concealed handgun permit holders in the United States have proven to be extremely law-abiding, losing their permits at only hundredths of thousandths of one percentage point for any type of firearms-related violation.

If dangerous weapons made citizens in other countries dangerous, no one would visit Switzerland. There, all able-bodied men between the ages of 20 and 42 are trusted to keep a machine gun in their homes as part of their military service. (Not the wimpy center-fire semi-automatic rifles everyone is afraid to trust Australians with.) Yet the trust in the Swiss is well placed. Switzerland has one of the lowest murder rates in Europe.

Letting law-abiding citizens in the U.S. and Switzerland own guns lowers crime because would-be victims are able to deter criminals or, if confronted, protect themselves. Australians are clearly quite different. They understand the risks of letting Australians own guns. The *International Crime Victimization Survey* shows that Australia's violent crime rate is already twice that of the United States or Switzerland. Australia's violent crime rate is about as high as England's, a country that bans handguns.

It would be simple enough just to blame Australia's high crime rates on its largely English heritage or its convict history, but for much of the past century Australia had lower crime rates than the US or the UK. Violent crime rates have gone up dramatically in Australia since the 1996 Port Arthur gun control measures. And violent crime rates averaged 20% higher in the six years after the law was passed (from 1997 to 2002) than they did in 1996, 32% higher than the violent crime rates in 1995. The same comparisons for armed robbery rates showed increases of 67% and 74%, respectively; for aggravated assault, 20% and 32%; for rape, 11% and 12%; murder, attempted murder and manslaughter rose by 5% in both cases.

Perhaps six years of crime data is just not enough to evaluate the experience. Yet Australian governments seem to believe that if gun controls don't work at first, more and stricter regulations (like getting rid of swords) are surely the solution. Remember, never second-guess government regulations.

While the ban on swords is modeled on the gun control measures, the Victorian Government obviously hopes that its new measure is more successful in reducing crime. Australian gun laws also require people to lock their guns in safes and ban many types of guns. But requiring an alarm for storing any swords, unlike the 15 or more rule for guns in Victoria, is a nice touch and may make the crucial difference.

Metal swords have been around since the Bronze Age, 4600 years ago. Yet citizens in few countries have so clearly posed dangers to themselves and it is fortunate that Victoria recognizes this.

Possibly, Australians can turn now to solving some really important problems. One suggestion: 240-volt electrical currents can kill you. Is it really true that Australians have these overpowering urges to try sticking metal in electrical sockets?

Originally appeared March 24, 2004 in The Australian.

Right-to-Carry Law is the Way to Go

While murder rates have been falling or have been flat for years in the rest of the country, Philadelphia's rate has been rising. Last year's murder rate was the highest since 1993, and Philadelphia replaced Chicago—the perennial leader—as the top 10 largest city with the highest murder rate. With 85 murders in the first 88 days of 2005, the city's murder rate is well ahead of even last year's.

Mayor John Street's solution? He's doing little about fixing the city's declining arrest rates for murder. Instead, he blames the law-abiding citizens who have permits to carry concealed handguns. He announced on Thursday that the city will deliberately begin delaying the issue of new concealed handgun permits. Governor Rendell's proposed crime task force promises to examine the issue further.

No reporters seem to have asked Street or Rendell the obvious question: If permit-holders are the problem, how many of those 85 murders were caused by a person with a permitted concealed handgun? When I asked, the city police and mayor's office were unable or unwilling to answer that question, but my guess is zero.

In the extraordinarily rare cases when permit-holders get in trouble, there is news coverage. Yet there's not one single news story on such a case this year.

Indeed, with 28,000 concealed handgun permit-holders in Philadelphia and more than 600,000 statewide, there was no such murder last year, or the year before, or the year before in the entire state. Only two have been recorded since the state law started in 1989.

Instead, in Philadelphia there are a number of cases such as this: Last December, a robber shot at a delivery man despite having taken all his money, and only then did the delivery man use his permitted concealed handgun to wound the robber.

There are dramatic cases statewide. A couple of years ago, a serial rapist in Pittsburgh was wounded by his sixth intended victim who had a permitted concealed handgun.

Pennsylvania's experience isn't unusual. Thirty-six other states have similar right-to-carry laws, and nine other states allow people to carry under more restrictive rules. In all of these cases, the type of person willing to take the time to apply for a permit and go through a criminal background check is extremely law-abiding. They lose their permits for any type of gun-related offenses at hundredths or thousandths of one percent.

Ohio, our most recent neighbor to adopt a right-to-carry law, adopted it almost a year ago. The *Akron Beacon Journal* reported last week that "some in law enforcement worried that routine traffic stops and road rage incidents would turn violent. That hasn't happened."

Similarly, in 2002, after Michigan's right-to-carry law had been in effect for a year, the *Detroit News* reported: "Such self-defense has not yet resulted in any kind of wave of new gun violence among those with fresh [concealed-weapon] permits, several law enforcement officials throughout Metro Detroit agreed."

Consider the two largest states with right-to-carry laws, Florida and Texas. During the 15 years after Florida's concealed-carry law took effect in October 1987, about 800,000 licenses were issued. Only 143 of these (two-hundredths of one percent) were revoked because of firearms-related violations. But even this statistic overstates the risks, as almost all of these cases apparently resulted from people simply accidentally carrying a gun into a restricted area, such as an airport.

The experience in Texas was similar. From 1996 through 1999, the first four years of Texas' concealed handgun law, 215,000 people were licensed. Data from the Texas Department of Public Safety showed that permit-holders were convicted of a crime only 6% as often as other adult Texans.

Police Commissioner Sylvester Johnson's claim that Pennsylvania has "the most lenient gun laws in the entire country" is simply incorrect. Several states don't even require a permit to carry a concealed handgun. Pennsylvania's law was modeled on Indiana's and is virtually identical to it. Pennsylvania is also one of 17 states that require background checks on even private transfers of guns.

Rendell favors adopting a limit of one gun a month. But no published academic studies show that such limits reduce any type of violent crime rate. If the state's gun laws are a problem, then why has Pittsburgh's murder rate fallen by 20 percent this year while Philadelphia's has increased?

As State Representative Dwight Evans, a Philadelphia Democrat, noted, "If Mayor Street thinks he's going to suddenly make street violence disappear by denying law-abiding citizens their right to self-defense, he's sadly mistaken." If Mayor Street is unwilling to protect Philadelphians by fixing the city's problems with law enforcement and lax judges, at least let law-abiding citizens protect themselves.

Originally appeared Mar. 29, 2005 in the Philadelphia Inquirer.

60 Minutes, Terrorists and Guns

Ironically, within a week of Dan Rather retiring from the CBS Evening News due to the fiasco over the *60 Minutes* Memogate scandal, this weekend *60 Minutes* was at it again, this time stirring up fears about how terrorists would use 50-caliber rifles to attack Americans.

Last year, the big fear was over the semi-automatic assault-weapons ban just before it expired. Senator Charles E. Schumer (D., N.Y.) claimed the ban was one of "the most effective measures against terrorism that we have." Of course, nothing happened when the law expired last year.

In the mid-1980s it was the hysteria over "plastic guns" when the Austrian company Glock began exporting pistols to the United States.

Now it is the 50-caliber rifles' turn, especially with California outlawing the sale of these guns since the beginning of the year. For years, gun-control groups have tried to ban 50-caliber rifles because of fears that criminals could use them. Such bans have not been passed—these guns were simply not suited for crime. Fifty-caliber rifles are big, heavy guns, weighing at least 30 pounds and using a 29-inch barrel. They are also relatively expensive. Models that hold one bullet at a time run nearly $3,000. Semi-automatic versions cost around $7,000. Wealthy target shooters and big-game hunters, not criminals, purchase them. The bottom line is that only one person in the U.S. has been killed with such a gun, and even that one alleged case is debated.

The supposed link to terrorism provides a new possible reason to ban 50-caliber rifles. *60 Minutes* darkly warned of ".50-caliber rifles, a gun that can kill someone from over a mile away and even bring down an airplane" and that "the bullets blew right through the steel plate." But the decision to demonize these particular guns and not say .475-caliber hunting rifles is completely arbitrary. The difference in width of these bullets is a trivial .025 inches. What's next? Banning .45-caliber pistols? Instead of protecting people from terrorists or criminals, the whole strategy is to gradually reduce the type of guns that people can own.

Sniper Central, a site for both military snipers and law-enforcement sharpshooters, claims that "For military extreme long-range anti-personnel purposes, the .338 Lapua is king. Even the .50BMG falls short. (Due to accuracy problems with current ammo)." The .338 Lapua round simply has what is called a better bullet coefficient, it produces less drag as it travels through the air.

With a 50-caliber rifle it is possible for an extremely lucky and skilled marksman to hit a target at 1,800 meters (versus 1,500 meters plus for the .338 Lapua), though most marksmen say that the effective range for any of these guns is around 1,000 meters. The reason is simple: to get these maximum distances, you can't fire directly at the target but must arc the shot at an angle. Bringing down an airplane with a semi-automatic rifle is very improbable.

Fighting terrorism is a noble cause, but the laws we pass must have some real link to solving the problem. As Dan Rather would say: "Courage."

Originally appeared March 25, 2005 in Tech Central Station.

Good Samaritan Gun Use

On February 24, 2005, a multiple victim public shooting outside the court house in Tyler, Texas—stemming from a custody dispute—resulted in the murder of two people and the wounding of four others.

Killings like this frequently make the news; this story was carried by all the television networks and most major newspapers. ABC and NBC evening news coverage was fairly typical; they noted, respectively, that "David Hernandez Arroyo fired off more than 50 rounds. He killed two people before police shot him dead" and "A gunman killed his ex-wife and a bystander and wounded four others between—before being shot to death by police."

Of the 71 unique news stories found by a computerized Nexis search of stories in the four days after the attack, 38% mention that an AK-47 or high-powered rifle was used by the attacker. As usual, gun control groups called for more gun control.

Eric Howard, with the Brady Campaign to End Gun Violence, said "These are military-style weapons that pose a significant risk to civilians and the police officers trying to protect the public."

Only two stories mentioned that the AK-47 was a semi-automatic, not a machine gun, and while it is understandable, none of the articles provided context by explaining that Arroyo's weapon functioned the same way as deer hunting rifles, firing the same caliber bullets at the same rapidity, causing the same damage.

Seems like pretty standard media coverage. But what makes this case different is that 21% of the news stories actually mentioned that a citizen licensed to carry a concealed weapon used his gun to try and help stop the attack.

The citizen, 50-year-old Mark Wilson, was one of the two people murdered. As CNN reported, "Everyone here agrees, Wilson saved lives." Fox News' website quoted the sheriff as saying "if it hadn't been for Mr. Wilson, [Arroyo's son] would be dead."

Wilson, a licensed concealed handgun permit holder, heard Arroyo's shots and saw the commotion from his apartment window. He grabbed a handgun and headed toward the attacker. Arroyo had already wounded several police officers and there was no one left to prevent his rampage.

Arroyo had also shot his 22-year-old son and was about to shoot him again at very close range when Wilson fired his gun, hitting Arroyo several times in the chest. Arroyo was wearing a bullet resistant vest and flak jacket and Wilson's shots did not seriously wound him. Yet Wilson's shots forced Arroyo to come after him, using up a couple of minutes of his time.

Unfortunately, in the exchange of gunfire, Arroyo fatally shot Wilson. With police arriving, Arroyo fled the scene and was later shot to death by police as they pursued him.

A neighbor described Wilson as "one of the nicest, sweetest guys I've ever known." Others pointed out that "He's not going to sit back and--when he could do something about it, and just let it happen" and called him a hero.

It is not remarkable that someone such as Mark Wilson was at the scene to stop the attack before police arrived. In about 30% of the multiple victim public school shootings since 1997 that have captivated Americans' attention, people used guns to stop the attacks before uniformed police were able to arrive on the scene. Few people know about these cases because only about 1% of the news stories on these cases mention how the attacks were stopped.

What is remarkable is that this heroism—an act of defensive gun use—did receive some national attention. Undoubtedly, much of the coverage came from the fact that Mark Wilson was killed by Arroyo, but it doesn't take away from the fact that many stories admitted that he had saved at least one life and a few stories quoted police saying that he had probably saved multiple lives.

Of course, gun control advocates draw their usual conclusion from all this. Kristen Rand, legislative director for the pro-gun control Violence Policy Center in Washington, D.C., claims the Tyler shooting last Thursday shows that criminals are undeterred by people potentially carrying concealed weapons. But, in fact, more nearly the opposite is true. When Arroyo faced the choice of continuing to shoot others or defending himself, he was forced to defend himself. Making Arroyo's attacks more risky caused him to change his behavior.

More generally, though, it is strange that Rand points to one case as evidence that deterrence doesn't work. In the book *The Bias Against Guns*, Bill Landes of the University of Chicago Law School and I examine multiple-victim public shootings in the United States from 1977 to 1999 and find that when states passed right-to-carry laws, these attacks fell by 60%. Deaths and injuries from multiple-victim public shootings fell on average by 78%.

Many people find it hard to believe that 18 national surveys by academics as well as national polling organizations show that there are 2 million defensive gun uses each year. After all, if these events were really happening, wouldn't we hear about them on the news? Yet when was the last time you saw a story on the national evening news (or even the local news) about a citizen using a gun to stop a crime? ABC's and NBC's news coverage continued this pattern, but at least some CBS and CNN news reports provided some balance and Fox News' website also gave the full story.

This misreporting endangers people's lives. By selectively reporting the news and turning a defensive gun use story into one that merely says "police shot him dead," the media give misleading impressions of what actions saved the lives of people confronted by violence. As Wilson's case demonstrates, defensive gun use is not a gun rights myth. Guns have been and are used by law abiding citizens to protect and save their own lives and the lives of others.

Originally appeared March 3, 2005 on FoxNews.com..

Banning Guns In the U.K. Has Backfired

Worried that even showing a starting pistol in a car ad might encourage gun crime in Britain, the British communications regulator has banned a Ford Motor Co. television spot because it pictures a woman holding such a "weapon." According to a report by *Bloomberg News*, the ad was said by regulators to "normalize" the use of guns and "must not be shown again."

What's next? Toy guns? Actually, this year the British government has been debating whether to ban toy guns. As a middle course, some unspecified number of imitation guns will be banned, and it will be illegal to take imitation guns into public places.

And in July a new debate erupted over whether those who own shotguns must now justify their continued ownership to the government before they will get a license.

The irony is that after gun laws are passed and crime rises, no one asks whether the original laws actually accomplished their purpose. Instead, it is automatically assumed that the only "problem" with past laws was they didn't go far enough. But now what is there left to do? Perhaps the country can follow Australia's recent lead and ban ceremonial swords.

Despite the attention that imitation weapons are getting, they account for a miniscule fraction of all violent crime (0.02%) and in recent years only about 6% of firearms offenses. But with crime so serious, the Labor Party needs to be seen as doing something. The government recently reported that gun crime in England and Wales nearly doubled in the four years from 1998-99 to 2002-03.

Crime was not supposed to rise after handguns were banned in 1997. Yet since 1996, the serious violent crime rate has soared by 69%; robbery is up by 45% and murders up by 54%. Before the law, armed robberies had fallen by 50% from 1993 to 1997, but as soon as handguns were banned the robbery rate shot back up, almost back to their 1993 levels.

The 2000 *International Crime Victimization Survey*, the last survey done, shows the violent-crime rate in England and Wales was twice the rate in the U.S. When the new survey for 2004 comes out, that gap will undoubtedly have widened even further as crimes reported to British police have since soared by 35%, while declining 6% in the U.S.

The high crime rates have so strained resources that 29% of the time in London it takes police longer than 12 minutes to arrive at the scene. No wonder police nearly always arrive on the crime scene after the crime has been committed.

As understandable as the desire to "do something" is, Britain seems to have already banned most weapons that can help commit a crime. It is hard to see how the latest proposals will accomplish anything.

Banning guns that fire blanks and some imitation guns. Even if guns that fire blanks are converted to fire bullets, they would be lucky to fire one or two bullets and would most likely pose more danger to the shooter than the victim. Rather than replace the barrel and the breach, it probably makes more sense to simply build a new gun.

Making it very difficult to get a license for a shotgun and banning persons under 18 from using shotguns also adds little. Ignoring the fact that shotguns make excellent self-defense weapons, they are so rarely used in crime, that the Home Office's report doesn't even provide a breakdown of crimes committed with shotguns.

Britain is not alone in its experience with banning guns. Australia has also seen its violent crime rates soar to rates similar to Britain's after its 1996 Port Arthur gun control measures. Violent crime rates averaged 32% higher in the six years after the law was passed (from 1997 to 2002) than they did the year before the law in 1995. The same comparison of armed robbery rates showed increases of 74%.

During the 1990s, just as Britain and Australia were more severely regulating guns, the U.S. was greatly liberalizing individuals' right to carry guns. Thirty-seven of the 50 states now have so-called right-to-carry laws that let law-abiding adults carry concealed handguns once they pass a criminal background check and pay a fee. Only half the states require some training, usually around three to five hours' worth. Yet crime has fallen even faster in these states than the national average. Overall, the states in the U.S. that have experienced the fastest growth rates in gun ownership during the 1990s have experienced the biggest drops in murder rates and other violent crimes.

Many things affect crime; the rise of drug-gang violence in Britain is an important part of the story, just as it has long been important in explaining the U.S.'s rates. Drug gangs also help explain one of the many reasons it is so difficult to stop the flow of guns into a country. Drug gangs can't simply call up the police when another gang encroaches on their turf, so they end up essentially setting up their own armies. And just as they can smuggle drugs into the country, they can smuggle in weapons to defend their turf.

Everyone wants to take guns away from criminals. The problem is that if the law-abiding citizens obey the law and the criminals don't, the rules create sitting ducks who cannot defend themselves. This is especially true for those who are physically weaker, women and the elderly.

Originally Published September 3, 2004 in Wall Street Journal Europe.

Gunning for Cheney

During the Vice Presidential debate, Senator John Edwards asked how Vice President Dick Cheney could possibly oppose laws such as one preventing "plastic" guns that can avoid metal detectors. The bill in question was written and supported by the NRA and supported by gun control groups. Senator Edwards implied that only someone far outside the mainstream could vote "no," and Edwards obviously wanted to use this vote to question Cheney's seriousness in dealing with terrorism.

Dick Cheney was one of only a handful of congressmen who voted against the bill when it came up in 1986. It was bad law. The law provided placebo cures for imaginary ills.

The hysteria over "plastic guns" arose in the mid-1980s when the Austrian company Glock began exporting pistols to the United States. Labeled as "terrorist specials" by the press, fear spread that their plastic frame and grip would make them invisible to metal detectors. Rarely mentioned was that Glocks still had over a pound of metal. Anyone who has ever been through a metal detector at an airport should understand how silly this fear was.

As Phillip McGuire, Associate Director of Law Enforcement of the Bureau of Alcohol, Tobacco and Firearms (BATF) testified at the time: "The entire issue was raised in response to reports, many wildly inaccurate, concerning a particular firearm, the Glock 17."

Despite all the horrible warnings about "plastic guns," Glocks are now common and there are good reasons they are one of the favorite pistols of American police officers. They are reliable and lightweight. No guns have ever been produced without metal in them, nor is there any evidence that such guns can be made. At the time of the vote in 1984, no gun had less than 3.5 ounces of metal.

So what did this supposedly crucial law do? It had nothing to do with Glocks. The minimum metal requirement for a gun to be considered legal was set at 3.2 ounces—less than a fifth of the metal contained in the then controversial Glocks and less than any other gun.

The standard was picked because it did not affect anything,

not because evidence suggested that some threshold was necessary for public safety. Gun control groups got their hysteria, while politicians were able to posture that they were "doing something."

During the 2000 election, Cheney was also attacked for his earlier vote on a bill concerning so-called "cop-killer" bullets, but the discussion was just as misleading. The bullet was invented by police officers in the 1960s to fire at suspects hiding behind objects or wearing bullet-resistant vests. These specialty bullets were only sold to police and were not available in stores anywhere in the United States. While often labeled "Teflon bullets," teflon had nothing to do with penetrating protective vests (the teflon simply helps reduce the abrasion to the gun's barrel). The important feature instead was their denser core, usually made out of tungsten.

Despite the phrase "cop-killer," only police used these bullets, and even then extremely rarely. Only one U.S. officer has ever been killed with such a bullet. The bill in question didn't even deal with bullets that might actually be used to penetrate bullet-resistant vests. Most rifle ammunition will do this; to have banned these bullets would have essentially outlawed most hunting.

As police know, there is still another irony attached to this discussion; unless the intended victim has protection, these bullets have less stopping power than hollow point bullets since they more easily pass through their victim and they are more likely than other bullets to wound than kill.

Just as with the law against "plastic" guns, this law changed nothing. Companies continued only selling these bullets to police.

Politicians often believe that it is important to "do something," even though that something often does nothing or makes things worse. It might be hard to understand that someone opposes laws that merely make you look like you care. Yet, when Cheney was challenged on this vote during the 2000 campaign, he told ABC's "This Week" that he takes seriously our country's bill of rights that state "the right to keep and bear arms shall not be infringed." Like many of his votes in congress, Cheney's votes made sense and required rare courage.

Originally appeared October 6, 2004 in Tech Central Station.

How Can Anyone Oppose Letting
Retired Police Carry Guns?

Chicago continues to have more murders than any other U.S. city -- a murder rate greater than any of the 10 largest cities in the country. Only five states have a higher murder rate than Illinois. Yet Governor Blagojevich, who faces a large state budget deficit, threatens to veto a bill which would allow retired police officers help patrol neighborhoods for free.

Illinois is one of only four states that do not trust retired police officers to carry guns. In fact, Illinois is one of only four states that ban every single citizen from carrying concealed handguns. The state Senate wants to change this situation, if only for police. By an overwhelming 40-12 vote, the Illinois Senate last week passed such a bill, though it still contained among the most stringent requirements anywhere. To get a permit a person must:

- have 10 years of experience as a police officer or as a military police officer
- have graduated from a police academy or training institute
- hold a valid firearm-owner's card

But how can anyone oppose letting retired police carry guns? We trust police when they are on the job. Research, including my own, shows that police are the single most important factor for reducing crime. But somehow, an officer we trusted for 10 years is no longer trusted the day he retires.

Blagojevich's concern? He claims that adopting the bill will lead "inexorably toward concealed carry laws" for all Illinois residents. Obviously, "slippery slopes" are not just the concerns of those who want to keep guns.

Don't worry though. Illinois isn't going to become like its neighbors—Indiana, Michigan, Kentucky, Missouri or Iowa—any time soon. Surely not another Indiana, where any law-abiding citizen 18 or older who passes a criminal background check and pays a $25 fee can carry a concealed handgun. Some 311,000 Indianans have permits, and no training is required.

One wonders how Blagojevich can sleep at night if he seriously worries that requiring 10 years as a police officer and graduation from a police academy is just a short step from letting anyone carry a concealed handgun with just a criminal background check.

Blagojevich's initial threats to veto any concealed carry bill for police changed this week to threatening a veto if military police veterans are allowed to carry guns. It is hard to take this new concern seriously. Besides the obvious safety record these military police have demonstrated with guns, probably no more than a thousand military veterans will even qualify to carry a concealed handgun, and it is safe to assume that only a fraction of those would bother to apply. Illinois has 1 million veterans, but only about 100,000 served for at least 10 years and fewer than 1 percent of soldiers would have served as military police for that whole period.

Exactly what Blagojevich is worried about seems a bit of a mystery, and his position on guns is changing daily. His flip-flops are not just limited to allowing police to carry guns. Over the last week, Blagojevich first supported lowering the age at which gun permits can be obtained, down to 18. Then—when gun control advocates got angry—he said he will support the bill only if a large number of semi-automatic handguns, rifles and shotguns were also banned. Of course, this is nothing new. As a congressman from Chicago, he had one of the most consistent gun control records in congress, but he ran for governor distributing camouflage-colored "Hunters for Blagojevich" bumper stickers and promising that he would be sensitive to their views on guns.

News reports quote gun-control advocates as saying Blagojevich is purposefully trying to complicate the gun issue so much that nothing passes, thus allowing Blagojevich "to blame a do-nothing legislature and claim to each side that he tried to champion their cause."

All this is a dangerous game. Today, even more than usual is at stake. Since September 11, terrorist threats have greatly increased the demands that states and cities cover all the possible vulnerable targets. The federal government advises us to be observant and report strange events to police. But there is not always time to call 911 and wait for the cavalry to arrive. With 40,000 to 50,000 retired local, state and federal law enforcement officers living in Illinois, this legislation could help provide well-trained individuals who may already be at the scene.

Blagojevich may honestly believe that political stalemate serves his interests, but murders and other violent crimes continue unabated.

Illinois does not let retired police to serve as unpaid undercover cops as they travel around town, nor does Illinois let citizens protect themselves. When will Chicago and the rest of Illinois realize that when you ban guns, it is the law-abiding citizens such as these retired cops—not the criminals—who obey the ban?

Originally appeared April 4, 2004 at Chicago Sun-Times.

Time to Level Playing Field for Gun Makers

Every product has illegitimate uses and undesirable consequences, but even lawsuits have had their limits. In 2002 in the U.S., car accidents killed 45,380 people and injured another 3 million, 838 children under the age of 15 drowned, 474 children died from residential fires, and 130 children died in bicycle accidents.

Fortunately, local governments haven't started recouping medical costs or police salaries by suing auto or bicycle companies, pool builders or makers of home heaters.

All sorts of products, including cars and computers, are also used in the commission of crimes. But again, no one yet seriously proposes that these companies be sued for the losses from these crimes.

People understand what makes a car useful for everyday life also makes it useful to escape a crime and that you can't hold a car company liable for a product that's working exactly as it should. They understand that the penalty should be on the person who uses the product improperly.

Yet suing manufacturers for the costs that cities incur from gun injuries and deaths is exactly the theory behind government lawsuits by cities against gun makers. George Soros, via the Brady Campaign, has funded most of these suits.

Last week, the House Judiciary Committee marked up their version of a bill to limit these suits, and the Senate will finally decide within the next couple of weeks whether these suits will continue. Last year, the "Protection of Lawful Commerce in Arms Act," an attempt to limit these suits, was defeated when Democrats added amendments to extend the so-called assault weapons ban.

Generally, suits against gun makers haven't had any more legal success than if similar suits had been brought against car companies. There have been some short term victories such as a decision last week by the D.C. Court of Appeals that will let the city sue makers of so-called "assault weapons" used in crime.

But while gun control advocates can dream about more such victories, the Brady Campaign had more practical goals: imposing large legal costs on gun makers. Even the largest gun companies make only a few million dollars in a good year. Those below the top 10 make just a few thousand guns a year and are usually family operations.

Obviously, bad things happen with guns. But the suits ignore that guns also prevent bad things by making it easier for victims to defend themselves. Unlike the tobacco suits, gun makers have powerful arguments about the benefits of gun ownership.

More than 450,000 crimes, including 10,800 murders, were committed with guns in 2002. But Americans also used guns defensively more than 2 million times that year, and more than 90 percent of the time merely brandishing the weapon was sufficient to stop an attack.

Police are important in reducing crime rates, but they virtually always arrive after a crime has been committed. When criminals confront people, resistance with a gun is by far the safest course of action. A 2004 survey found that 94% of 22,600 chiefs and sheriffs questioned thought that law-abiding citizens should be able to buy guns for self-defense.

My own research has found that increased gun ownership rates are associated with lower crime rates. Poor people in the highest crime areas benefit the most from owning guns. Lawsuits against gun makers will raise the price of firearms, which will severely reduce gun ownership among the law-abiding, much-victimized poor.

Advocates for these suits claim that the gun makers make their weapons attractive to criminals through low price, easy concealability, corrosion resistance, accurate firing and high firepower. Lightweight, concealable guns may help criminals, but they also have helped protect law-abiding citizens and lower crime rates in the 46 states that to varying degrees allow concealed handguns.

Women benefit most and also find it easier to use smaller, lightweight guns. Poor victims benefit more than wealthier ones from the ability to protect themselves simply because they are more likely to be victims.

Some suits seek to hold gun makers liable because accidental deaths are "foreseeable" and not enough was done to make guns safe. Nationally, 31 children under 10 and 71 children under 15 died from accidental gun deaths in 2001. Yet with some 90 million people owning more than 260 million guns, accidental deaths from guns are far less "foreseeable" than from many other products. Most gun owners must be very responsible or such gun accidents would be much more frequent.

Attempts to have the court system ignore a product's benefits to society are bad enough. Even worse is the cynical attempt to file bogus lawsuits simply to impose massive legal costs and eventually try bankrupting legitimate companies.

Passing the "Protection of Lawful Commerce in Arms Act" this month would still allow suits but would put gun makers on the same legal footing as other American manufacturers.

Originally appeared April 26, 2005 in Investors' Business Daily.

Gun Control Remains a Loaded Issue for Democratic Candidates: The Rhetoric May be Toned Down, but the Aim Remains the Same

with Grover Norquist

Everyone seems to believe that Democrats have changed their minds on gun control. Out on the campaign trail, John Kerry and John Edwards and Wesley Clark talk about their boyhood hunting trips. Before the Iowa caucuses, Kerry even took time out to shoot a pheasant. The gun control organization Americans for Gun Safety calls it "taking the gun issue to the political center." The National Rifle Association's leader, Wayne LaPierre, claims that "the center of the party saw that [advocating gun control] was a dead end for the Democrats." And Newsweek spread the word: "At least among the presidential candidates," said an article in January, "Democrats are moderating their stances" on gun control.

If one reads the candidates' public statements on the 2nd Amendment, they certainly seem moderate:

Kerry: "I believe that the Constitution, our laws and our customs protect law-abiding American citizens' right to own firearms. I believe that the right of gun ownership comes with responsibilities."

Howard Dean: "Law-abiding citizens should have the right to own firearms for hunting and other legitimate purposes, subject to reasonable restrictions related to gun safety."

Edwards: "I believe that the 2nd Amendment protects Americans' right to own firearms for purposes like hunting and personal protection, and that this right is subject to responsible limits like other rights."

The uniformity of views is striking, as are the "reasonable restrictions" the major Democratic candidates support: banning so-called semiautomatic assault weapons, regulating gun shows, opposing restrictions on lawsuits against gun makers.

Given all this agreement, it is not surprising that last year Democratic pollster Mark Penn produced surveys showing that if Democrats didn't show "respect for the 2nd Amendment and support gun safety," voters would presume that they were anti-gun. "The formula for Democrats," according to Penn, "is to say that they support the 2nd Amendment, but that they want tough laws that close loopholes. This is something [Democrats] can run on and win on." Remember, Bill Clinton and Democratic strategists are on the record as saying that too strong a stand for gun control probably cost Al Gore the 2000 presidential elections.

But is the conversion real? The policy gurus for the Democratic presidential campaigns recently pitched their candidates at a think-tank breakfast in Washington. Given their candidates' stated support for the right of individuals to own guns, where do they draw the line on reasonable restrictions? Where do they stand on, say, the bans on handgun ownership in Chicago and the District of Columbia?

Only Joe Lieberman's representative answered the question. The now-former Democratic candidate "would oppose an outright ban on handguns, and he is not afraid to say so." And the others? Dean's senior advisor, Maria Echaveste, refused to be pinned down because that would be giving in to "wedge issue" politics "as opposed to really talking about values that are fundamental to all candidates and to the American people." Representatives for Kerry, Edward and Clark would not respond.

The question was hardly theoretical. A couple of weeks ago, a U.S. District Court judge, a Democratic appointee, ruled in a District of Columbia case upholding the district's ban: "The 2nd Amendment does not confer an individual a right to possess firearms. Rather, the amendment's objective is to ensure the vitality of state militias."

Just last month, a man in Wilmette, Illinois—where there is also a handgun ban—used a gun to stop a criminal breaking into his home while his family slept. Police said that in wounding the perpetrator, the homeowner used justifiable force and that the handgun met state regulations for being registered and properly stored, but the man was charged with violating Wilmette's ban. He had previously called 911 to report a break-in at his home and had to wait more than 10 minutes for police, but in the second case, with the criminal staring at him, he didn't have the luxury of waiting that long again.

Supporting "reasonable restrictions" sounds moderate, but is an ownership ban "reasonable"? And if so, what exactly does guaranteeing an individual right really mean?

Polling may have convinced Democrats to change their rhetoric, but when only one Democratic presidential candidate—one no longer running—"would oppose an outright ban on handguns," their true goals must be as extreme as ever.

Originally appeared February 6, 2004 at Los Angeles Times.

Athletes and Guns

Giant NFL players admitting they feel threatened by crime? This hardly fits their tough, macho image. Our concern is supposed to be for women walking alone at night.

But while the massive size and strength of NFL players might seem to make them unlikely victims, their wealth and high profiles nonetheless make them targets for violent criminals. Yet crimes against professional athletes don't engender much sympathy or news coverage.

So, what do many NFL players do when they realize that their physical strength does not give them enough protection from violent crime? The same as many other would-be victims—they get guns. Well over 50% of NFL players are estimated to own guns. By contrast, about 45% of American adults generally own guns. Shortly before New Year's, the concern that a majority of NFL players actually own guns rated a news story in the politically correct *New York Times*.

Early in the morning on January 21, Corey Fuller, the 5-foot 10-inch, 210-pound defensive back for the Baltimore Ravens, was confronted by two armed robbers outside his Tallahassee house. One robber chased Fuller into his house where his wife and children were sleeping, but Fuller was able to grab a gun and fire at the attackers, who then ran away.

In late October, T.J. Slaughter, a 6-foot, 233-pound linebacker, was arrested for allegedly pointing a gun at motorists who pulled up next to him on the highway. Slaughter denied that he had pointed the gun at the motorists and claimed that they had threatened him. According to Slaughter, he told the men to move away from his car. No charges were filed, but the Jacksonville Jaguars still cut Slaughter the next day. Jacksonville claimed Slaughter was performing poorly.

Greg Anthony, a 6-foot, 176-pound guard for 12 years in the NBA, carried a registered gun during part of his career. He said, "More and more people approach you, and you just never know what somebody is capable of doing ... [Players] see carrying as a deterrent."

Well-known coaches, such as Barry Switzer and Bobby Knight, have also carried guns.

Recent media stories—from the *New York Times* to the *Chicago Tribune*—have run extremely negative stories on professional players owning guns. The *Tribune* described players owning guns as a "problem [that] persists." Ironically, within days of the December *New York Times* piece, it was revealed that the *New York Times* lets its reporters carry guns in Iraq.

With high profile basketball players including Allen Iverson, Charles Barkley and Scottie Pippen having been arrested for illegal gun possession—as well as football players such as Alonzo Spellman and Damien Robinson—the issue of professional athletes and guns is often in the news, and this coverage helps form people's opinions. (Though, in all these cases, charges were eventually dropped.)

There are no systematic numbers on the crimes committed against professional athletes, but anecdotal stories abound, proving that professional athletes' physical strength hardly makes them immune to crime. Take the following examples, for instance:

• Yancy Thigpen of the Tennessee Titans (height: 6-1, weight: 203 lbs.) has faced three armed robberies since joining the NFL eight years ago. The last one left him and his fiancée tied up inside his house with their 2-month old daughter locked in a closet. An earlier robbery involved a carjacking.

• Will Allen of the New York Giants (height: 5-10, weight: 195 lbs.) was assaulted, doused with gasoline and robbed by an assailant when he returned to his house one evening in 2001.

Unfortunately all of the nation's four leading pro sports leagues—the National Football League, the National Basketball Association, the National Hockey League and Major League Baseball—trivialize the athletes' safety concerns. The NFL's official advice: "In some circumstances, such as for sport or protection, you may legally possess a firearm or other weapon. However, we strongly recommend that you not do so." The league advocates passive behavior when confronted by a criminal.

Such misguided advice simply makes players and their families more vulnerable and does not square with the U.S. Department of Justice's findings. The Justice Department's *National Crime Victimization Survey* has shown for decades that providing no self-protection is among the actions most likely to result in injury. Even actions other than carrying a weapon are safer than passive behavior.

The NFL has gone so far as to conduct annual seminars for their athletes on firearms, stressing the risks to children of guns and the risks of having a gun in a car. The teams have forbidden players from having guns with them at stadiums or while traveling on League-related business, but this leaves players who obey the rules as sitting ducks before or after games.

Indeed, the players who violate the rules are probably doing their teammates a favor because they at least create some uncertainty in criminals' minds about whether a player can protect himself. Yet the league's sanctions make players reticent to talk about defensive gun uses.

Even professional athletes are not supermen. T. J. Slaughter expresses no regrets for having a gun despite running afoul of political correctness and being cut by the Jaguars. He said. "I believe legally owning a gun is the right thing to do. It offers me protection. I think one day it could save my life." It seems a lesson that many who are not quite as strong can learn from.

Originally appeared January 28, 2004 at Foxnews.com.

P.C. Air Security: When Will Our Pilots Be Armed?

It has been almost two years since 9/11 and recent news headlines warn "Al Qaeda May Be Planning More Hijack Attacks." Unfortunately, our air-travel system is still very vulnerable to hijacking, and quick measures need to be taken. Another successful attack would make it very difficult to again restore travelers' faith in security.

Last week, pilots from around the country held rallies in Atlanta, Chicago, Dallas, Los Angeles, Miami, and Washington, D.C. to draw attention to their concerns.

Pilots claim that while at least one third of flights out of Washington's Reagan National are covered with air marshals, the rest of the country is being ignored. Only a small fraction of flights to Europe are being covered and then only one day a week.

The newest generation of reinforced cockpit doors was put in place in April, but few experts have much faith in their effectiveness. Last summer, on a bet, a cleaning crew rammed a drink cart into one of the new doors on a United Airlines plane. The door reportedly broke off its hinges.

No tests of airport screening have been made public since the government took over screening last fall, but, in private meetings that I have attended, the Transportation Security Administration (TSA) acknowledges there is a wide range of undetectable lethal weapons.

For example, without full-body searches there is no way to detect ceramic or plastic knives that are taped to an inside thigh. People who have flown can readily understand that while the checks are troublesome, they are simply not patted down all over their body. Unless you are going to do full-body searches on people, determined terrorists are going to be able to get weapons on planes no matter how carefully screeners monitor x-ray machines and metal detectors.

THE COSTS

Despite the gaps, these three programs have proven to be very costly. Potential cuts in airport screeners have generated a great deal of concern. Mentions of possible financial problems involving the marshals program have also been in the news.

Yet, with the ineffectiveness of screeners and so few marshals, such cuts do not pose the real threat. In terms of cost effectiveness it is hard to think of a policy that produces the ratio of benefits to costs that arming pilots has. For example, the only real financial cost to the government for pilots involves a one-week training class. Even then pilots are training on their own time. There are none of the salaries required for marshals or screeners once the training is completed.

Only $8 million of the $5 billion available to TSA for airline security is being spent on arming pilots. A five-fold increase in expenditures on arming pilots would reduce other expenditures by only about 1%.

UNDERMINING THE PROGRAM

Unfortunately, despite Homeland Security Secretary Tom Ridge recently voicing public support for arming pilots, TSA has fought the program at every turn. After two years since the first attacks and two laws passed overwhelmingly by Congress to start training pilots, only about 200 out of over 100,000 commercial passenger pilots are licensed to carry guns.

Following what seemed like a successful first class of pilots this spring, TSA fired the head of the firearms training academy, Willie Ellison, for "unacceptable performance and conduct."

Ellison, who won the praise of the students, was reprimanded for holding a graduation dinner for the first graduation class and giving them baseball caps with the program logo.

The training facility was closed down and relocated immediately after the first class, prompting Oregon Representative Peter DeFazio, the ranking Democrat on the Aviation Subcommittee, to complain that the closing appeared to be "just another attempt to disrupt the program."

On top of all the delays, the administration has done what it can to discourage pilots from even applying for the armed-pilot program.

The intrusive application form pilots are required to fill out warns them that the information obtained by TSA is "not limited to [the pilot's] academic, residential, achievement, performance, attendance, disciplinary, employment history, criminal history record information, and financial and credit information."

The information can be turned over to the Federal Aviation Administration (FAA) and used to revoke a pilot's commercial license. As one pilot told me, "The Transportation Security Administration is viewed as hostile to pilots, and pilots are afraid that if they are not viewed as competent for the [armed-pilots] program, they may be viewed as not competent to continue being pilots."

The screening and psychological testing required of the pilots are also much more extensive and intrusive than that required for the vast majority of air marshals who are currently on duty. Some questions even appear designed to purposefully disqualify pilot applicants.

About half the pilots applying for the program were rejected in the initial screening process. No explanations for those rejections have been provided, making the entire system unaccountable.

In the last week or so, TSA apparently has come to reconsider some of those rejections and called pilots to tell them that the decisions had been made too quickly. But with all the secrecy surrounding the process, it is impossible to evaluate whether those who continue to be rejected deserve to be. It is hard to think of any reason why the applicant can't be told even in even the most general way the basis for rejections. The initial high rates of rejection have certainly put a chill on applications.

HARDLY EXPERIMENTAL

Despite the concerns about hypothetical risks, arming pilots is not some new experiment. About 70% of the pilots at major American airlines have military backgrounds, and military pilots flying outside the U.S. are required to carry handguns with them whenever they flew military planes.

Until the early 1960s, American commercial passenger pilots on any flight carrying U.S. mail were required to carry handguns. The requirement started at the beginning of commercial aviation to insure that pilots could defend the mail if their plane were to ever crash.

In contrast to the current program, there were no training or screening requirements. Indeed, pilots were still allowed to carry guns until as recently as 1987. There are no records that any of these pilots (either military or commercial) carrying guns have ever caused any significant problems.

TYPICAL OBJECTIONS

Many concerns have been raised about arming pilots or letting them carry guns, but armed pilots actually have a much easier job than air marshals. An armed marshal in a crowded cabin can be attacked from any direction; he must be able to quickly distinguish innocent civilians from terrorists.

An armed pilot only needs to concern himself with the people trying to force their way into the cockpit. It is also much easier to defend a position such as the cockpit, as a pilot would, than to have to pursue the terrorist and physically subdue them, as a marshal would. The terrorists can only enter the cockpit through one narrow entrance, and armed pilots have time to prepare themselves as hijackers try to penetrate the strengthened cockpit doors.

Pilots must also fly the airplane—but with two pilots, one pilot would continue flying the plane while the other defended the entrance. In any case, if terrorists are in the cockpit, concentrating on flying will not be an option.

An oft-repeated concern during the debate over arming pilots is that hijackers will take the guns from them, since "21% of [police] officers killed with a handgun were shot by their own service weapon." Similar concerns are frequently raised when discussing civilians using guns for their personal protection. But the Federal Bureau of Investigation's (FBI) Uniform Crime Report paints a quite different picture. In 2000, 47 police officers were killed with a gun, out of which 33 cases involved a handgun, and only one of these firearm deaths involves the police officer's gun.

It is really not that easy to grab an officer's gun and shoot him. Assaults on police are not rare, but only in a miniscule fraction of assaults on officers do officers end up losing control and being shot with their own gun. Statistics from 1996 to 2000 show that only eight thousandths of one percent of assaults on police resulted in them being killed with their own weapon.

The risk to pilots would probably be even smaller. Unlike police who have to come into physical contact with criminals while arresting them, pilots will use guns to keep attackers as far away as possible.

Unable to accept pilots carrying guns, the administration continues to float suggestions for Tasers (stun guns) instead of guns, ignoring their limitations. Not only are there well-known cases (such as that of Rodney King, who "fought off Tasers" twice), but thick clothing can also foil their effectiveness. The New York City Police Department reports that: "Even Taser guns—which the department uses to administer electric shocks to people—fail about a third of the time." Because of these problems, even the Taser manufacturer recommends lethal weapons as a back up. Use against terrorists would be even less reliable since terrorists would prepare in advance to wear clothing or take other precautions to protect themselves from stun guns.

The fears of having guns on planes are exaggerated. Ron Hinderberger, Director of Aviation Safety at Boeing, noted in testimony before the U.S. House of Representatives that Boeing commercial service history contains cases where guns were fired on board in service airplanes, all of which landed safely.

Commercial airplane structure is designed with sufficient strength, redundancy, and damage tolerance that a single or even multiple handgun holes would not result in loss of an aircraft. A bullet hole in the fuselage skin would have little effect on cabin pressurization. Aircraft are designed to withstand much larger impacts whether intentional or unintentional. For instance, on 14 occasions Boeing commercial airplanes have survived, and landed, after an in flight bomb blast.

SKY MILES YET

The Bush administration can hardly claim confidence that its screening, reinforced doors and air marshals are enough. A successful attack will make it very difficult for the government to restore travelers' confidence for years. The damage to the airline industry would be even greater than after the first attack.

Protecting people should be as important as protecting the mail once was.

Originally appeared September 2, 2003 in the National Review.

Half Cocked: Why Most of What You See in the Media About Guns is Wrong

I often give talks to audiences explaining that research by me and others shows that guns are used much more often to fend off crimes than to commit them. People are very surprised to learn that survey data show that guns are used defensively by private citizens in the U.S. anywhere from 1.5 to 3.4 million times a year. A question I hear repeatedly is: "If defensive gun use occurs so often, why haven't I ever heard of even one story?"

Obviously, anecdotal stories published in newspapers can't prove how numerous these events are, but they can at least deal with the question of whether these events even occur. During 2001, I did two detailed searches on defensive gun uses: one for the period covering March 11 to 17 of that year, and another for the period July 22 to 28. While these searches were not meant to be comprehensive, I found a total of 40 defensive gun uses over those two weeks. Some representative examples:

• Clearwater, Florida: At 1:05 a.m., a man started banging on a patio door, beat on a family's truck, then tore open the patio door. After numerous shouted warnings not to break into the home, a 16-year-old boy fired a single rifle shot, wounding the attacker.
• Columbia, South Carolina: As two gas station employees left work just after midnight, two men attempted to rob them, beating them about the head and neck with a shovel handle. The male employee broke away long enough to draw a handgun from his pocket and shot at his attacker, who later died.
• Detroit, Michigan: A mentally disturbed man wailed that the President was going to have him killed and started firing at people in passing cars. A man at the scene who had a permit to carry a concealed handgun fired shots that forced the attacker to run away.
• West Palm Beach, Florida: After being beaten during a robbery at his home, a home owner began carrying a handgun

in his pocket. When another robber attacked him just two days later the homeowner shot and wounded his assailant.

• Columbia Falls, Montana: A woman's ex-boyfriend entered her home to sexually assault her. She got away long enough to get her pistol and hold her attacker at gun point until police arrived.

• Baton Rouge, Louisiana: At 5:45 a.m., a crack addict kicked in the back door of a house and charged the homeowner, who shot him to death.

• Gainesville, Florida: A newspaper carrier was dragged from his car and beaten by five men at 3:15 a.m. The victim then shot one of the attackers in the chest with a concealed weapon.

• Tampa, Florida: Two teenage armed robbers went on a four-hour crime spree, hijacking cars, robbing people, and hospitalizing one victim with serious injuries. They were stopped when one intended victim, a pizza-store owner, shot and wounded one attacker.

• Charleston, South Carolina: A carjacking was stopped by a 27-year-old victim who then shot one of his attackers. The victim had paused to ask directions when several men, one with a lengthy criminal record, jumped into the car.

These life and death stories represent only a tiny fraction of defensive gun uses. A survey of 1,015 people I conducted during November and December of 2002 indicates that 2.3 million defensive gun uses occurred nationwide in 2001. Guns do make it easier to commit bad deeds, but they also make it easier for people to defend themselves when few alternatives are available. That is why it is so important that people receive an accurate, balanced accounting of how guns are used. Unfortunately, the media are doing a very poor job of that.

Though my survey indicates that simply brandishing a gun stops crimes 95% of the time, it is very rare to see a story of such an event reported in the media. A dead gunshot victim on the ground is highly newsworthy, while a criminal fleeing after a woman points a gun is apparently not considered news at all. That's not impossible to understand; after all, no shots were fired, no crime was committed, and no one is even sure what crime would have been committed had a weapon not been drawn.

In other words, airplane crashes get news coverage, while successful take-offs and landings do not. Even though fewer than one out of 1,000 defensive gun uses result in the death of the attacker, the newsman's penchant for drama means that the bloodier cases are usually covered. Even in the rare cases where guns are used to shoot someone, injuries are about six times more frequent than deaths. You wouldn't know this from the stories the media choose to report.

But much more than a bias toward bad news and drama goes into the medias selective reporting on gun usage. Why, for instance, does the torrential coverage of public shooting sprees fail to acknowledge when such attacks are often aborted by citizens with guns? In January 2002, a shooting left three dead at the Appalachian Law School in Virginia. The event made international headlines and produced more calls for gun control.

Yet one critical fact was missing from virtually all the news coverage: The attack was stopped by two students who had guns in their cars.

The fast responses of Mikael Gross and Tracy Bridges undoubtedly saved many lives. Mikael was outside the law school returning from lunch when Peter Odighizuwa started shooting. Tracy was in a classroom waiting for class to start. When the shots rang out, chaos erupted. Mikael and Tracy were prepared to do something more constructive: Both immediately ran to their cars and got their guns, then approached the shooter from different sides. Thus confronted, the attacker threw his gun down.

Isn't it remarkable that out of 208 news stories (from a Nexis-Lexis search) in the week after the event, just four mentioned that the students who stopped the shooter had guns? A typical description of the event in the *Washington Post*: "Three students pounced on the gunman and held him until help arrived." New York's *Newsday* noted only that the attacker was "restrained by students." Many stories mentioned the law-enforcement or military backgrounds of these student heroes, but virtually all of the media, in discussing how the killer was stopped, said things such as: "students tackled the man while he was still armed," "students tackled the gunman," the attacker "dropped his gun after being confronted by students, who then tackled him to the ground," or "students ended the rampage by confronting and then tackling the gunman, who dropped his weapon."

In all, 72 stories described how the attacker was stopped, without mentioning that the heroes had guns. Yet 68 stories provided precise details on the gun used by the attacker: The *New York Times* made sure to point out it was "a .380 semiautomatic handgun"; the *Los Angeles Times* noted it was "a .380-caliber semiautomatic pistol."

A week and a half after the assault, I appeared on a radio program in Los Angeles along with Tracy Bridges, one of the Appalachian Law School heroes. Tracy related how "shocked" he had been by the news coverage. Though he had carefully described to over 50 reporters what had happened, explaining how he had to point his gun at the attacker and yell at him to drop his gun, the media had consistently reported that the incident had ended by the students "tackling" the killer. When I relayed what the *Washington Post* had reported, Tracy quickly mentioned that he had spent a considerable amount of time talking face-to-face with reporter Maria Glod of the *Post*. He seemed stunned that this conversation had not resulted in a more accurate rendition of what had occurred.

After finishing the radio show, I telephoned the *Washington Post*, and Ms. Glod confirmed that she had talked to both Tracy Bridges and Mikael Gross, and that both had told her the same, story. She said that describing the students as pouncing, and failing to mention their guns, was not "intentional." The way that things had come out was simply due to space constraints.

I later spoke with Mike Getler, the ombudsman for the *Post*. Getler was quoted in the *Kansas City Star* as saying that the reporters simply did not know that bystanders had gotten their guns. After informed him that Glod had been told by the students about using their guns, yet excluded that information, Getler said that she "should have included it." However, Getler said that he had no power to do anything about it. He noted that readers had sent in letters expressing concern about how the attack had been covered. But none of these letters was ever published.

The *Kansas City Star* printed a particularly telling interview with Jack Stokes, media relations manager at the Associated Press, who "dismissed accusations that news groups deliberately downplayed the role gun owners may have played in stopping" the shooting. But Stokes "did acknowledge being 'shocked' upon learning that students carrying guns had helped subdue the gunman. 'I thought, my God, they're putting into jeopardy even more people by bringing out these guns.'"

Selective reporting of crimes such as the Appalachian Law School incident isn't just poor journalism; it could actually endanger people's lives. By turning a case of defensive gun use into a situation where students merely "overpowered a gunman" the media give potential victims the wrong impression of what works when confronted with violence. Research consistently shows that having a gun (usually just showing it) is the safest way to respond to any type of criminal assault.

It's no wonder people find it hard to believe that guns are used in self-defense 2 million times a year: Reporting on these events is systematically suppressed. When was the last time you saw a story in the national news about a private citizen using his gun to stop a crime? Media decisions to cover only the crimes committed with guns--and not the crimes stopped with them—have a real impact on people's perceptions of the desirability of guns.

To flesh out this impression with some data, I conducted searches of the nation's three largest newspapers—*USA Today*, the *Wall Street Journal*, and the *New York Times*—for the year 2001 and found that only the *Times* carried even a single news story on defensive gun use. (The instance involved a retired New York City Department of Corrections worker who shot a man who was holding up a gas station.) Broadening my search to the top ten newspapers in the country, I learned that the *Los Angeles Times*, *Washington Post*, and *Chicago Tribune* each managed to report three such stories in a year.

To gain further perspective, I conducted deeper searches comparing the number of words newspapers published on the use of guns for committing crimes versus stopping crimes. For 2001, I found that the *New York Times* published 104 gun-crime news articles—ranging from a short blurb about a bar fight to a front-page story on a school shooting—for a total of 50,745 words. In comparison, its single story about a gun used in self-defense amounted to all of 163 words. *USA Today* contained 5,660 words on crimes committed with guns, and not a single word on defensive gun use. The least lopsided coverage was provided by the *Washington Post*, with 46,884 words on crimes committed with guns and 953 words on defensive stories—still not exactly a balanced treatment.

Moreover, the few defensive news stories that got coverage were almost all local stories. Though articles about gun crimes are treated as both local and national stories, defensive uses of guns are given only local coverage in the rare instances they run at all. In the full sample of defensive gun-use stories I have collected, less than 1% ran outside the local coverage area. News about guns only seems to travel if it's bad.

This helps explain why residents of urban areas are so in favor of gun control. Most crime occurs in the biggest cities, and urbanites are bombarded with tales of gun-facilitated crime. It happens that most defensive gun uses also occur in these same big cities, but they simply aren't reported.

This imbalance isn't just limited to newspapers. Take the 1999 special issue of *Newsweek* entitled "America Under the Gun." Though over 15,000 words and numerous graphics were provided on the topic of gun ownership, there was not one mention of self-defense with a firearm. Under the heading "America's Weapons of Choice," the table captions were: "Top firearms traced to crimes, 1998"; "Firearm deaths per 100,000 people"; and "Percent of homicides using firearms." Nothing at all on "Top firearms used in self-defense," or "Rapes, homicides, and other crimes averted with firearms." The magazine's graphic, gut-wrenching pictures all showed people who had been wounded by guns. No images were offered of people who had used guns to save lives or prevent injuries.

To investigate television coverage, I collected stories reported during 2001 on the evening news broadcasts and morning news shows of ABC, CBS, and NBC. Several segments focused on the increase in gun sales after September 11, and a few of these shows actually went so far as to list the desire for self-defense as a reason for that increase. But despite slightly over 190,000 words of coverage on gun crimes, merely 580 words, on a single news broadcast, were devoted to the use of a gun to block crime—a story about an off-duty police officer who helped stop a school shooting. Not one of the networks mentioned any other defensive gun use, and certainly not one carried out by a civilian.

Another place where the predilections of reporters color the news about guns is in the choice of authorities quoted. An analysis of *New York Times* news articles over the last two years reveals that Times reporters overwhelmingly cite pro-gun-control academics in their articles. From February 2000 to February 2002, the *Times* cited nine strongly pro-control academics a total of 20 times; one neutral academic once; and no academic who was skeptical that gun control reduces crime. Not once. The same pro-control academics were referenced again and again: Philip Cook of Duke, Alfred Blumstein of Carnegie Mellon, Garen Wintemute of the University of California at Davis.

This imbalance in experts interviewed cannot be explained away by an inability to find academics who are dubious about most gun control laws. Two hundred ninety-four academics from institutions as diverse as Harvard, Stanford, Northwestern, the University of Pennsylvania, and UCLA released an open letter to Congress in 1999 stating that the new gun laws being proposed at that time were "ill advised." These professors were economists, lawyers, and criminologists. None of these academics was quoted in *New York Times* reports on guns over a two-year period.

Polls frequently serve as the basis of news stories. While they can provide us with important insights about people's views, polls can also mislead in subtle ways. In the case of weapons, poll questions are almost always phrased with the assumption that gun control is either a good thing or, at worst, merely ineffective. The possibility that it could have bad results and even increase crime is never acknowledged. Consider these questions from some well-known national polls:

• Do you think that stricter gun control laws would reduce the amount of violent crime in this country a lot, a little, or not at all? (Pew Research Center/*Newsweek*)

• Do you think stricter gun control laws would reduce the amount of violent crime in this country, or not? (ABC News/*Washington Post*)

• Do you think stricter gun control laws would, or would not reduce violent crime? (CBS News)

I reviewed 17 national and seven state surveys and found that all asked only whether gun control laws reduce crime; not one offered respondents a chance to consider whether gun control might increase crime. This notion apparently never entered the pollsters' minds.

The omission in such polls of a "would increase crime" option creates a bias in two different ways. First, there is an "anchoring" effect. We know that the range of options people are offered in a poll affects how they answer, because many respondents instinctively choose the "middle ground." By only providing the choices that gun control reduces crime somewhere between "a lot" to "not at all," the middle ground becomes "a little."

Second, when the possibility that gun control could cause crime is removed from polls, this affects the terms of national debate. When people who hold this view never even hear their opinions mentioned in polls and news stories, they begin to think no one else shares their view. Repeated surveys that imply gun control either makes society better or has no impact gradually acculturate Americans to accepting the view that is constantly presented.

There are other subtle biases in the construction of these surveys. When a survey questions whether gun control will be "very important" for the respondent at the voting booth, the media often hear a "yes" answer as evidence that the person wants more gun control. Rarely do they consider that someone might regard a politician's position on gun control as important because he or she opposes it. This same blurring of opposite positions in one question causes gun control to be ranked more highly as an election issue than it should be. Polls typically compare issues such as "increased defense spending" (which captures supporters on just one side of the issue) with questions on "gun control" (where both anti- and pro-control partisans say the issue is important, yet believe entirely different things).

A final area strongly affected by the media's anti-gun bias is that of accidental shootings. When it comes to this, reporters are eager to write about guns. Many have seen the public service ads showing the voices or pictures of children between the ages of four and eight, implying that there is an epidemic of accidental deaths of these young children.

Data that I have collected show that accidental shooters overwhelmingly are adults with long histories of arrests for violent crimes, alcoholism, suspended or revoked drivers licenses, and involvement in car crashes. Meanwhile, the annual number of accidental gun deaths involving children under ten—most of these being cases where someone older shoots the child—is consistently a single digit number. It is a kind of media archetype story, to report on "naturally curious" children shooting themselves or other children, though from 1995 to 1999 the entire United States saw only between five and nine cases a year where a child under ten either accidentally shot themselves or another child.

The danger of children stumbling across guns pales in comparison to many other risks. Over 1,260 children under ten died in cars in 1999. Another 370 died as pedestrians hit by cars. Accidents involving residential fires took 484 children's lives. Bicycles are much more likely to result in accidental deaths than guns. 93 children under the age of ten drowned accidentally in bathtubs. 36 children under five drowned in buckets during 1998. In fact, the number of children under ten who die from any type of accidental gunshot is smaller than the number of toddlers who drown in buckets. Yet few reporters crusade against buckets or bathtubs.

When crimes are committed with guns, there is a somewhat natural inclination toward eliminating all guns. While understandable, this reaction actually endangers people's lives because it ignores how important guns are in protecting people from harm. Unbalanced media coverage exaggerates this, leaving most Americans with a glaringly incomplete picture of the dangers and benefits of firearms. This is how the media bias against guns hurts society, and costs lives.

Originally appeared July 1, 2003 in The American Enterprise.

The Ban Against Public Safety: D.C. Gun Laws Have Increased Crime

with Eli Lehrer

Since 1976, Washington D.C. residents have lived under the nation's most restrictive gun laws; Police enforce a citywide handgun ban, and local statutes require residents to keep long guns disassembled, unloaded and locked up. The law even forbids target shooting. Those who envision the United States as a violent cowboy nation might take comfort in knowing that this regime offers more restrictions than the laws anywhere else in the United States, in Canada, or indeed, in any major European Union nation.

Even in a nation where many see gun ownership as a birthright, D.C.'s gun-control, in effect since 1976, aroused surprisingly little controversy until recently. Had the law worked, the relative lack of controversy wouldn't surprise anyone. But, instead, the law hasn't done anything to reduce violence. Last year, the District, never far out of the running, reclaimed the title of the U.S. murder capital among the 30 most populous cities.

Now, a full-scale effort to challenge the law has gotten underway. Gene Healy and Robert Levy, both employees of the libertarian Cato Institute but acting for themselves, have filed a lawsuit challenging the D.C. law on Second Amendment grounds, and Senator Orrin Hatch (R-Utah) has introduced legislation to overturn it. "It is time to restore the rights of law-abiding citizens to protect themselves and to defend their families against murderous predators," says Mr. Hatch. The two Cato staffers think much the same way. "Why should we say to people who work hard and live by the rules that they can't protect themselves?" asks Mr. Healy.

And D.C. residents need more protection: Crime has risen significantly since the gun ban went into effect. In the five years before Washington's ban in 1976, the murder rate fell from 37 to 27 per 100,000. In the five years after it went into effect, the murder rate rose back up to 35. In fact, the murder rate after 1976 has only once fallen below what it was in 1976. Robberies and overall violent crime changed just as dramatically. Robberies fell from 1,514 to 1,003 per 100,000 and then rose by over 63 percent, up to 1,635. These drops and subsequent increases were much larger than any changes in neighboring Maryland and Virginia. For example, the District's murder rate fell 3.5 to 3 times more than that of its neighboring states and rose back 3.8 times more.

The District does face some severe crime problems unrelated to the gun ban. Although it has improved in recent years, the District's police force still fights a legacy of corruption and incompetence: Under city hiring rules police can't use even basic intelligence tests to screen applicants. Department computer systems don't work and officers sometimes have trouble finding functional patrol cars. During the early 1990s, as Congress demanded that the city improve police staffing, the city failed to conduct even basic background checks. As a result, at least 50 officers still on the force and subject to civil service protections have criminal records so severe that they cannot work the streets or testify in court. The city's poor neighborhoods, likewise, rank among the worst in the country, and community-police cooperation suffers just about everywhere.

But even cities with far better police agencies have seen crime soar in the wake of handgun bans. Chicago, which has banned all handguns since 1982, has police computer systems that are the envy of the nation, a bevy of shiny new police facilities and a productive working relationship with community groups. Indeed, the city has achieved impressive reductions in property crime in recent years. But the gun ban didn't work at all when it came to reducing violence. Chicago's murder rate fell from 27 to 22 per 100,000 in the five years before the law and then rose slightly to 23.

The change is even more dramatic when compared to five neighboring Illinois counties: Chicago's murder rate fell from being 8.1 times greater than its neighbors in 1977 to 5.5 times in 1982, and then went way up to 12 times greater in 1987. While robbery data isn't available for the years immediately after the ban, since 1985 (the first year for which the Federal Bureau of Investigation has data) robbery rates soared.

In other words, crime rates actually improved prior to these bans and then deteriorated after they took effect. Even though guns will leak into the District and Chicago from neighboring areas, at least some minor benefit still should have been observed if gun bans reduce crime. Instead, the opposite was the case. The gun bans appear to have disarmed only law-abiding citizens while leaving criminals free to prey on the populace.

Originally appeared August 11, 2003 in The Washington Times.

Right to Carry Would Disprove Horror Stories

Governor Bob Holden finally vetoed the right-to-carry legislation last week, expressing fears about the risks the law poses for police and children.

With more than 70% of the Missouri House and Senate already voting for the bill, the expected veto override battle appears to be coming down to a single vote in the Senate.

Gun control advocates such as Holden are right to fear the right-to-carry bill's passage, but not for the reason that most people think. Despite panicked claims that innocent people will be killed and there will be shootouts in the streets, here is a prediction: A year after enactment Missouri's newspapers will report that all the horror stories about letting citizens carry concealed handguns were wrong. The real loser will be gun control advocates' credibility.

My prediction does not really involve going out on a limb. The bill allows trained, law-abiding citizens to carry concealed handguns for their protection, and Missouri's law will be the most restrictive right-to-carry law in the nation.

One needs only to look at the other 32 states with right-to-carry laws where we have had enough time to see what happens. A year after the law goes into effect, newspaper articles in state after state announce that the supposed fears never materialized. It is particularly hard to see why these worries are taken seriously in Missouri, four of whose neighbors have right-to-carry laws.

Michigan, the most recent state to have a right-to-carry law in effect for at least a year, adopted it in 2001. Last year newspapers such as the *Detroit News* regularly reported that: "Such self-defense has not yet resulted in any kind of wave of new gun violence among those with fresh...permits, several law enforcement officials throughout Metro Detroit agreed."

And consider the two largest states with right-to-carry laws, Florida and Texas. In the 15 years after Florida's concealed-carry law took effect in October 1987, about 800,000 licenses were issued. Only 143 of these (two-hundredths of 1%) were revoked because of firearms-related violations.

But even this statistic overstates the risks, as almost all of these cases apparently resulted from people accidentally carrying a gun into a restricted area, such as an airport. No one claims that these unintentional violations posed any harm. In general, permit-holders were model law-abiders. Even off-duty police officers in Florida were convicted of violent crimes at a higher rate than permit-holders.

The experience in Texas was similar. From 1996 through 1999, the first four years that Texas' concealed-handgun law was in effect, 215,000 people were licensed. Permit holders turned out to be law-abiding, with licensees convicted of a crime only 6% as often as other adult Texans.

Data for other states are also available and paint a similar picture. It is not surprising that no state with a right-to-carry law has repealed it.

One particular fear raised by Holden is that right-to-carry laws would actually make police officers' jobs more dangerous by making it more likely that they would be shot. Yet research has shown that the laws make police safer. Professor David Mustard of the University of Georgia found that right-to-carry laws reduced the rate that officers were killed by about 2% per year for each year that the laws were in effect. Several studies find that as law-abiding citizens are allowed to defend themselves, criminals are much less likely to carry guns. Fewer criminals carrying guns makes the jobs of police less dangerous.

While Missouri's police organizations are generally neutral, national surveys show that police support concealed handgun laws by a 3-1 majority. Many former strong opponents of right-to-carry laws across the country have changed their positions after the laws have been in effect for a couple of years.

Glenn White, president of the Dallas Police Association, provides a typical response: "I lobbied against the law in 1993 and 1995 because I thought it would lead to wholesale armed conflict. That hasn't happened....I think it's worked out well, and that says good things about the citizens who have permits. I'm a convert."

When he vetoed the right-to-carry bill, Holden also claimed that right-to-carry laws would increase accidental shootings, but there is not one academic study that finds that to be true. For violent crime, refereed academic studies range from showing that right-to-carry laws at worst have little or no benefit to most research finding large reductions that increase as more permits are issued.

A year after the right-to-carry law is enacted, Missourians will wonder what all the fuss was about. Those declaring that Missourians' safety is endangered will lose credibility once people see that it is criminals and not law-abiding citizens who have the most to fear from Missourians' being able to defend themselves.

Originally appeared July 12, 2003 in The Kansas City Star.

United Nations vs. Guns:
An International Gun-Control Fight

The U.S. government often makes American gun owners feel besieged. For example, over the last decade it is simply impossible to find one study by either the U.S. Justice Department or the Treasury that measures the benefits of gun ownership. While this has been done by both Democratic and Republican administrations, the Clinton administration surely set new standards for misleading attacks on gun ownership with its studies and public-service ads.

But if you think that is bad, the Clinton administration pales in comparison to the United Nations' (UN) attitude on gun ownership. This week the UN conference to "Prevent, combat, and eradicate the Illicit Trade in small arms and Light Weapons in All Aspects," which concludes today, puts these views in straightforward terms: Governments have the "right" to guns for "self defense and security needs." On the other hand, not one acceptable reason for individuals owning guns is mentioned. And to the extent that individuals do buy guns, third-world and western European countries are pushing for a tax on every gun purchase, with the money then being used to eliminate world hunger.

WHEN GOVERNMENTS ARE A THREAT

The UN claims that guns used in armed conflicts cause 300,000 deaths worldwide every year. The solution proposed in conference's "Program of Action"? Keep rebels from getting guns by requiring that countries "prevent, combat and eradicate" what those countries who want to stop rebels from getting the guns define as "the illicit trade in small arms."

This may be an understandable "solution" from governments that don't trust their citizens. But it also represents a dangerous disregard for their citizens' safety and freedom. Why? First, and most obviously, because not all insurgencies are "bad." It is hardly surprising that infamous regimes such as those in Syria, Cuba, Rwanda, Vietnam, Zimbabwe, and Sierra Leone support these "reforms." To ban providing guns to rebels in totalitarian countries is like arguing that there is never anything such as a just war.

In hindsight, would Europeans have preferred that no resistance was put up against Hitler? Should the French or Norwegian resistance movements simply have given up? Surely this would have minimized war causalities.

Many countries already ban private gun ownership. Rwanda and Sierra Leone are two notable examples. Yet, with more than a million people hacked to death over the last seven years, were their citizens better off without guns?

Political scientist Rudy Rummel estimates that the 15 worst regimes during the 20th century killed 151 million of their own citizens. Even assuming that the 300,000-gun-deaths-per-year-in-armed-conflicts figure is accurate, the annual rate of government-sanctioned killing is five times higher. Adding the UN's estimated deaths from gun suicides, homicides, and accidents still provides a number that is only a third as large.

Of course, this last numerical example is questionable as gun control is more likely to increase than reduce violent crime. To put it in its most extreme form, suppose that tomorrow guns were banned, who would be most likely to turn them in? Presumably the most law-abiding citizens—not the criminals. And my own research shows that disarming law-abiding citizens relative to criminals emboldens the criminals to commit crimes.

What about the massacre of civilians in Bosnia? Would that have been so easy if the Bosnian people had been able to defend themselves? And what about the Jews in the Warsaw ghetto during World War II? Wouldn't it have been better if they had more guns to defend themselves? More recently, the rules would have prevented the American government from assisting the Afghanis in their fight against the Soviet Union.

There is a second reason to avoid a ban on small arms. Even in free countries, where there is little risk of a totalitarian regime, gun bans almost invariably result in higher crime. In the U.S., the states with the highest gun-ownership rates have by far the lowest violent-crime rates. And similarly, over time, states with the largest increases in gun ownership have experienced the biggest drops in violent crime.

Research by Jeff Miron at Boston University, examining homicide rates across 44 countries, found that countries with the strictest gun-control laws also tended to have the highest homicide rates. News reports in Britain showed how crimes with guns have risen 40% in the four years after handguns were banned in 1997. Police are extremely important in stopping crime, but almost always arrive on the scene after the crime occurs. What would the UN recommend that victims do when they face criminals by themselves? Passive behavior is much more likely to result in serious injury or death than using a gun to defend oneself.

TAXING GUN SALES

Brazil's President Liz Inacio Lula da Silva advocated the arms-sales tax as a way that the world's wealthy nations could eliminate world hunger. French President Jacques Chirac immediately said, "Lula's idea is a simple one. People must be able to eat three times a day, and that is not the case today." Elsewhere Chirac has also called the tax on guns "quite justified."

Yet, this tax makes about as much sense as taxing medicine to help feed the poor. One would think that the rest of the world would understand that the police simply cannot be there all the time to protect people. The 2000 International Crime Victimization Survey shows that almost all the western countries in their survey have much higher violent crime rates than the U.S., including Australia, Canada, Denmark, England/Wales, Finland, France, Netherlands, New Zealand, and Sweden. (Jeff Miron argues that the relatively high murder rate in the United States is driven not by our gun-ownership rate but by gang violence that results from our drug-enforcement regulations.)

The Bush administration deserves credit for stopping the 2001 UN conference from implementing many of the same proposals that are still being pushed now. One thing you can say about those united nations: They sure are persistent.

Originally appeared July 11, 2003 in the National Review Online.

Armed, and Safer, Iraqis

The June 14 deadline for Iraqi citizens to turn in banned weapons worked about as poorly as any gun buy-back program in the United States. After the two-week program ended, a guard at one of the designated places to turn in guns said, "We have had plenty of reporters, but no weapons come in."

American soldiers are laying down their lives to protect Iraqi citizens, and the last thing that we want to do is put them in harm's way. On Tuesday, six British soldiers were killed. During the preceding week, an American soldier was killed by a sniper and another killed in a drive-by shooting.

But as we try to protect Iraqis and ensure the safety of our troops, we must ask: Is it really clear that our soldiers are better off by attempting to disarm Iraqi citizens?

The argument seems straightforward enough: Get rid of guns, and the Iraqis can't harm our troops. Banning the carrying of guns also makes it easier for soldiers to simply arrest anyone they are suspicious of.

But the question is more complicated: If guns are banned, who would turn them in? Presumably the most law-abiding citizens, not the terrorists and Ba'ath Party members our troops should be concerned about.

Fortunately, despite many news stories to the contrary, our government has taken a much more sensible approach than banning guns outright. Iraqis are able to keep weapons up to AK-47s in their home or business and are able to carry guns with them with a permit. These AK-47s are real military machine guns, not the semi-automatic versions that fire only one bullet per trigger pull and are banned from being sold in our country by the 1994 so-called assault-weapons ban. Yet despite Iraqis owning machine guns and the country still not under control, Defense Secretary Donald Rumsfeld pointed out that Baghdad is experiencing fewer murders than Washington, D.C., where handguns are banned.

To the extent that guns are banned and law-abiding citizens disarmed, the jobs for our soldiers actually become more difficult.

Crime is already rampant. Consider the case of Mohammed Abdul Razak, an Iraqi taxi driver who lost his handgun when soldiers stopped him at a checkpoint because he had it in his car's glove compartment without the proper permit.

Just two days later, Razak could not defend himself when carjackers attacked. Before his gun was taken, Razak had successfully used his gun to scare off thieves.

As one report recently noted: "Instead of being filled with people coming to give up their guns, police stations are busy with Iraqis complaining about being victims of crime—as well as people who say they want their confiscated weapons back." A machine gun can be handy to defend oneself when people are being attacked by bands of thugs.

It would be great if gun-control laws primarily disarmed criminals, but as data from the U.S. and other countries indicates, disarming law-abiding citizens actually increases crime and encourages criminals to attack because they have less to worry about. Studies continually show that gun-control laws such as gun buy-backs, waiting periods, one-gun-a-month regulations, assault-weapons bans and gun-show regulations are associated with either no statistically significant change or increases in violent crime. The states that polls show as having the biggest increases in gun ownership are also the ones that have experienced the biggest relative drops in violent crime.

But won't letting citizens carry weapons make soldiers' jobs more difficult and more dangerous? Surely it is easy to imagine what can go wrong when a soldier comes across a citizen with a gun.

Yet recent research by Professor David Mustard at the University of Georgia examined jurisdictions with different kinds of gun laws and found that only one kind was associated with fewer police being killed by criminals - the kind that lets citizens carry concealed handguns. The people who take the time to apply for a permit to carry a gun are not the people police have to worry about. Interestingly enough, criminals apparently become less likely to carry guns as more law-abiding citizens do so.

With an American media that reports only the bad things that happen with guns, it might be hard for some Americans to understand that the simplistic approach of banning guns can make our soldiers' jobs more difficult. Our soldiers are extremely important in creating a stable society, but they cannot protect more than 22 million Iraqis all of the time. Wasting resources on collecting Iraqi guns will only work against efforts to make Iraq eventually a civilized country.

Originally appeared June 26, 2003 in the New York Post.

Bad Sports:
A Church Turns Down $10,000
from Sportsmen

When should a modest local church turn down $10,000 a year for sports activities that help keep children off the streets and out of gangs? Apparently, that will happen this coming Saturday when the money is raised by the Catholic Sportsmen's Organization by raffling off a shotgun.

John Aquilino wanted to do something to replace the tattered uniforms of the Hyattsville, Maryland Catholic Youth Organization sports teams. New basketball uniforms hadn't been purchased for nine years. The blue-collar area also had numerous other pressing problems: The convent roof was leaking, the parochial school was recently fined $4,000 for faulty fire doors, and the school's carpet was decrepit. Unfortunately, ordinary raffles for things like the sports teams were only raising about a couple hundred dollars.

With St. Jerome's Catholic Church located only a ten-minute or so trip from the Prince George's County Trap and Skeet Center, Aquilino hit upon the idea of shooting contests and a gun raffle each year on the Saturday before Father's Day. It has been a roaring success, raising thousands of dollars just its first year. New uniforms were purchased and money was provided for new carpeting at the school.

Opponents of the raffle and skeet shoot sprang up as soon as the idea was discussed. Aquilino offered opponents a challenge to see whether their approaches would raise as much money. One woman answered the challenge and set up bingo contests (and in the spirit of friendly competition, the "gun nuts" helped her out a lot a long the way). Starting three years ago, right when the Catholic Sportsmen's Organization started, she has raised about a quarter of the money raised by the sportsmen. But this was a contest where everyone won. As Aquilino said, "I think that it is great, that is $8,000 [raised by the bingo games] the kids didn't have."

To Peggy Alexander, a former member of the church, "it's a moral issue. It's about putting more guns out on the street. It's against the life-affirming doctrine that the Catholic Church preaches."

So far, the winners of the raffle during the first three years hardly fit that dangerous image: a choir master at a neighboring parish, a 70-year-old mother of one of the people who helps out at the church, and the general counsel for NASA.

Surely no one wants criminals to get guns. But few criminals participate in church fundraisers or pass background checks and the evidence is that with over two million defensive guns uses each year, guns are used at least four times more frequently to stop crime than they are used to commit it.

The most vulnerable in our society, those who are weaker physically, such as women and the elderly, as well as poor people (particularly blacks) who are most likely the victims of violent crime benefit the most from owning guns. Police are extremely important in stopping crime (my own research indicates that they are the single most important factor), but they understand that they can't be everywhere all the time and that they almost always arrive on the scene after the crime has been committed. The Catholic Church clearly recognizes the right of self defense, and telling people to behave passively turns out not to be very safe advice.

Unfortunately, Theodore Cardinal McCarrick, the archbishop of Washington, has tried to stop the raffles and skeet shoots. The cardinal decided that the sportsmen's group could only raise money for the church as long as it was not "related in any way to the use or sale of guns."

This hasn't satisfied opponents, who worry that some of the "tainted money" could still find its way into church coffers. They also complain that the "Sportsmen's group members wear t-shirts with gun images to church events."

The media hasn't missed the chance to paint gun owners as uncaring cavemen. The *Washington Post* paints the disagreement as being between "some people [who] cannot get beyond their fascination with guns and some people [who] actually believe the words of their faith's commandments." That good intentions might be on both sides never seems to have crossed liberal minds.

Originally appeared October 28, 2002 in The National Review.

Scare Tactics on Guns and Terror

Who could oppose laws preventing terrorists from getting guns? Obviously, no one. But it would be nice if these laws accomplished something more than simply making it more difficult for Americans to own guns.

Last week, the Congressional Research Service issued an alarming report claiming that international terrorists can easily exploit U.S. gun laws. Senator Lautenberg had requested the report. Unfortunately, the report simply lists possibilities that are often impossible or only remotely plausible.

The report points to loopholes in existing laws such as allowing "official representatives of a foreign government" possession of a firearm if necessary to their official capacity. Similar loopholes are pointed out for other "officials of foreign governments" who have the permission of their governments, need it for their official duties, and who have been residents in a state for at least 90 days.

Of course, such attacks using government agents is not what al Qaeda has been doing, nor is there any evidence that foreign government officials are currently planning such attacks. But if a foreign government plans on using diplomatic cover to engage in terrorism, surely just banning such officials from buying guns in the US won't stop them from getting access to guns. What is the solution? Full body searches of foreign diplomats entering the US? Searches of all diplomatic poaches?

The report mentions threats from "semi-automatic assault weapons" and 50-caliber "sniper rifles." Yet these banned semi-automatic assault weapons are not machine guns. They function exactly the same as other semi-automatic guns and fire one bullet per pull of the trigger. The banned guns are the same as other non-banned semi-automatic guns, firing the exact same bullets with the same rapidity. Forcing gun makers to change the name of their gun or changing cosmetic features, such as a bayonet mount, have nothing to do with terrorism.

The assault weapons ban has been in effect for almost a decade, but there is still not one study showing that it reduced any type of violent crime. No studies indicate that similar state laws, such as New Jersey's 1990 law, have also not reduced violent crime.

The report's alarm about terrorists getting guns at gun shows is just as misleading. As evidence of this threat, the report cites a Florida newspaper story claiming that members of Hezbollah were convicted of a variety of firearms violations for attempting to smuggle firearms purchased at a Michigan gun show out of the country. Unfortunately, none of the laws being advocated by the Senator would actually have been relevant here. A Lebanese citizen did try to illegally ship two shotguns to Lebanon. However, the guns were purchased by the Lebanese citizen's brother, a naturalized American citizen—not a foreign terrorist. While shipping the two shotguns broke export regulations, the supposed link with Hezbollah was never made.

Given that gun shows account for such a trivial share of guns obtained by criminals—less than one percent—and there is not even anecdotal evidence that the laws would have stopped terrorism, the proposals seem to be all cost and no benefit. Empirical work that I have done indicates that the types of regulations advocated by the report would reduce the number of gun shows by between about 14 and 24%.

Fighting terrorism is a noble cause, but the laws we pass must have some real link to solving the problem. Absent that, many will think that Senator Lautenberg is simply using terrorism as an excuse to promote rules that he previously pushed. Making it difficult for law-abiding Americans to own guns should not be the only accomplishment of new laws.

Originally appeared May 30, 2003 in The Star-Ledger.

When Gun Laws Don't Make Sense

Everyone seems to agree that it was an accident. A judge dismissed charges calling it just that. Yet, Anthony Sarkis' excellent teaching record did not protect his job at the Shaler Area High School. The school board voted unanimously to fire the teacher because of the zero tolerance ban on weapons at school. Sarkis' violation: he had accidentally brought a loaded handgun in a backpack to school.

In a public education system where elementary students are suspended from school for pointing a pencil and saying "pow" or facing criminal charges for playing cops and robbers during recess, Sarkis' firing is hardly surprising. And none of the apologies that he has offered will ever be viewed as sufficient.

Surely, banning guns near schools is meant to create a "safe zone" for our children, but does putting up a sign that reads "This is a Gun-Free Zone" make children safer? Not many people would put a sign up on their home saying: "This Home is a Gun-Free Zone." Why? Would doing so actually discourage criminals who threatened your family from entering your home?

The answer seems pretty obvious. Such "safe zones" simply mean that criminals have a lot less to worry about. Indeed, international data as well as data from across the United States indicate that criminals are much less likely to attack residents in their homes when they suspect that the residents own guns.

In the massive news coverage of public school shootings, what the media seldom mentions is how frequently attacks were stopped— long before the police arrived—by a citizen with a gun. One of these was the October 1997 shooting spree at a high school in Pearl, Mississippi that left two students dead. An assistant principal ran over a quarter of a mile to retrieve a gun from his car and then ran back. At point blank range he held the shooter at gun point for over five minutes while waiting for the police.

The school-related shooting in Edinboro, Pennsylvania that left one teacher dead was halted only after a bystander pointed a shotgun at the shooter when he started to reload his gun. The police did not arrive for another 11 minutes.

An off-duty police officer used his gun to help end an attack at a Santee, California school. Last year, a shooter at the Appalachian Law school in Virginia was stopped when two students retrieved their handguns from their cars.

Who knows how many lives were saved by these prompt responses?

Yet, anecdotal stories are not sufficient to resolve this debate. My book, *The Bias Against Guns*, examines all the multiple-victim public shootings occurring in the U.S. from 1977 to 1999. A range of different gun laws, such as waiting periods background checks, and assault weapon bans, as well the frequency and level of punishment were studied; However, while arrest and conviction rates, prison sentences, and the death penalty reduce murders generally, these laws have had no significant effect on public shootings. There is a simple reason for this: those who commit these crimes usually die. They are killed in the attack or they commit suicide. The normal penalties are simply not relevant.

To stop these attacks, we must learn what motivates these particular sorts of killers. In their deranged minds, their goal is to kill and injury as many people as possible. Only one policy can stop these attacks and thus reduce multiple victim shootings: the passage of right-to-carry laws.

The impact of these laws, which give adults the right to carry concealed handguns—if they do not have a criminal record and pay a fee—is very dramatic. Twenty-three states adopted these laws during the period studied. When the laws were adopted, the number of multiple-victim public shootings declined by 68%. Deaths and injuries from these shootings plummeted by about 80%. Most importantly for Sarkis' case, to the extent that attacks still occur in states after these laws are enacted they disproportionately occur in those areas in which concealed handguns are forbidden—the so-called gun free "safe zones."

Citizens with concealed handguns also have an important advantage over uniformed police in that would-be attackers can either aim their initial assault at the officer or wait until he leaves the area. With concealed handgun laws, it is also not necessary that many people even carry a weapon. In a public setting, with many people present, the probability that at least one person will be able to respond to an attack is extremely high.

Federal law has prohibited guns within 1000 feet of a school since 1995. Yet, even advocates of so-called gun free "safe zones" will be hard pressed to claim that it has produced the desired results. These are mindless laws, enforced with zero tolerance for the facts of cases such as Anthony Sarkis'.

Originally appeared April 2, 2003 in The Pittsburgh Tribune-Review.

Bullets and Bunkum:
The Futility of "Ballistic Fingerprinting"

In the wake of the Washington, D.C., sniper attacks, many are viewing ballistic fingerprinting as a magic crime-solving tool. According to the pro-gun-control Brady Campaign, such a system "would have solved [the sniper case] after the first shooting"; a *Washington Post* columnist calls it a "common-sense measure"; and many politicians are jumping on board, including New York Democratic senator Charles Schumer and Maryland Democratic gubernatorial nominee Kathleen Kennedy Townsend. Unfortunately, the issue is not so simple; by draining resources away from other police activities and making it costly for law-abiding citizens to own guns, ballistic fingerprinting could end up actually increasing crime.

The physics of ballistic fingerprinting are straightforward. When a bullet travels through the barrel of a gun, the friction creates markings on the bullet. If the gun is new, imperfections in the way the barrel is drilled can produce different markings on the bullet; such imperfections are most noticeable in inexpensive guns. (This poses an irony for gun controllers, who push for laws that ban inexpensive guns.) In older guns, the bullets' friction through the barrel can cause more noticeable wear marks that help differentiate between guns. Many other factors influence the particular markings left on the bullets—for instance, how often the gun is cleaned and what brand of cartridge is used.

Precisely because friction causes wear, a gun's ballistic fingerprint changes over time, making it drastically different from forensic evidence like human fingerprints or DNA. The recording of a child's fingerprints or DNA allows for identification much later in life; the same is not true of the bullet markings. A ballistic fingerprint is less like a human fingerprint than it is like the tread on a car tire.

Brand-new tires are essentially identical, so new-tire tracks at crime scenes leave investigators with pretty limited information. Unless there happens to be a particular imperfection, only the brand and model of the tire can be identified. Imprints on bullets are similar. When a bullet is fired from a new gun, investigators can typically identify only the type of ammunition and the type of gun. Over time, though, friction causes the tread on tires to wear. It would be easy to take the tire tracks left at a crime scene and match them with a suspected criminal's car; but the more the car is driven after the crime, the harder it is to match the tire tracks left at the scene to the tires when they are eventually found. Similarly, the greatest friction on a gun occurs when the gun is first fired - and that dramatically reduces the usefulness of recording the gun's ballistic fingerprint when it is purchased.

Moreover, ballistic fingerprinting can be thwarted by replacing the gun's barrel, just as criminals can foil tire-matching by simply replacing their tires. In general, the markings on bullets can be altered even more quickly and easily than the tread marks on tires; scratching part of the inside of a barrel with a nail file would alter the bullet's path down the barrel and thus change the markings. So would putting toothpaste on a bullet before firing it.

Ballistic fingerprinting faces other difficulties. For example, even if the gun was not used much between the time the ballistic fingerprint was originally recorded and the time the crime occurred, police still have to be able to trace the gun from the original owner to the criminal. Only 12% of guns used in crime are obtained by the criminal through retail stores or pawn shops; the rest are virtually impossible to trace.

So far, only Maryland and New York have started recording the ballistic fingerprints of all new handguns sold. While Maryland's program technically started in January 2001, the cost of implementing the program made it unprofitable for gun makers to sell handguns in the state for the first six months of that year. The state government faced a $1.1 million start-up cost and another $750,000-a-year operating cost. New York's program began in March 2001, with a state start-up expenditure of about $4.5 million. (No estimates are available yet on New York's annual cost.)

In both states, the costs for dealers, gun makers, and prospective gun owners were responsible for reducing handgun sales to law-abiding citizens. And what was the specific benefit? Almost zero. The programs have not helped solve a single violent crime in either state; they have so far been used only to identify two handguns stolen from a Maryland gun shop.

A recent study by the State of California points to further practical difficulties with ballistic fingerprinting. The study tested 790 pistols firing a total of 2,000 rounds. When the cartridges used with a particular gun came from the same manufacturer, computer matching failed 38 percent of the time. When the cartridges came from different manufacturers, the failure rate rose to 62 percent. And this study does not even begin to address problems caused by wear, so the real-world failure rate can be expected to be much higher. The California report warned that "firearms that generate markings on cartridge casings can change with use and can also be readily altered by the users." Further, it warned that the problems of matching would soar dramatically if more guns were included in the sample. The study's verdict: "Computer-matching systems do not provide conclusive results . . . potential candidates [for a match must] be manually reviewed."

While registering guns by their ballistic fingerprints is a relatively new concept, we have had plenty of experience using gun registration in general, and it has come up woefully short. A couple of years ago, I testified before the Hawaii state legislature on a bill to change registration requirements. Hawaii has had both registration and licensing of guns for several decades.
In theory, if a gun is left at the crime scene, licensing and registration will allow the gun to be traced back to its owner. Police have probably spent hundreds of thousands of man-hours administering these laws in Hawaii. But despite this massive effort, there has not been a single case in which police claimed that licensing and registration have been instrumental in identifying a criminal.

The reason is simple. First, criminals very rarely leave their guns at a crime scene, and when they do, it is because the criminals have been killed or seriously wounded. Second—and more important for ballistic fingerprinting—would-be criminals also virtually never get licenses or register their weapons. The guns that are recovered at the scene are not registered.

Good intentions don't necessarily make good laws. What counts is whether the laws actually work, and end up saving lives. On that measure, ballistic fingerprinting—a useless diversion of valuable police resources—fails conspicuously, and it should be opposed by anyone who wants to live in a safer society.

Originally appeared November 11, 2002 in The National Review.

Democrats Have Not Dropped Gun Control Agenda

Has the gun control issue really disappeared? Some think that Democrats, chastised by the loss of the presidency of 2000 and the loss of the Senate in 2002, have learned the risk of supporting gun control the hard way. Some even argue that there is a more fundamental change in Democratic beliefs on gun control.

Yet, as Democratic House leader Nancy Pelosi recently said, Democrats will wait and revisit the guns "when the issue is ripe."

New regulations are still being put forward, but legislation gets more attention—both from the press and other legislators—when there is a chance it will pass. There is surely no shortage of new gun control proposals at either the federal or state level.

• Assault Weapons Ban. In Congress, House Democrats are pushing for a vastly expanded ban (including all semi-automatic shotguns that are widely used for hunting and skeet shooting) that, among other features, gives future U.S. Attorney Generals the ability to ban any semi-automatic rifle they classify as not for "sporting" uses. Senate Democrats propose slightly expanding the ban only because they acknowledge that their most desired legislation would never get passed.

• Judicial Appointments. Just last week, Alabama Attorney General Bill Pryor, a Republican nominated by President Bush for a judgeship on the 11th Circuit Court of Appeals, was criticized by Senate Democrats for supporting a court decision that requires judges to hold a hearing before they can order a person's gun be taken away.

• Filibusters. Senate Democrats threaten to filibuster legislation designed to rein in abusive litigation targeting the firearms gun makers. The suits threaten the very existence of gun makers; lawsuits have already forced several gun manufacturers into bankruptcy, some before they even had their day in court. While moderate Democrats support the bill, most Democratic Senators appear willing to fight against this to the very end.

• New Federal Regulations. In June, Senator Jon Corzine and Representative Patrick Kennedy, both Democrats, put forward legislation giving the Department of Justice sweeping powers to regulate the design, manufacture and distribution of guns. Just at the end of May, Senator Frank Lautenberg proposed banning large caliber guns and other new rules that regulate who can buy guns at gun shows.

• New State Regulations. From gun storage laws in New York to taxing gun show transfers in Illinois to banning large caliber guns in California to fining parents whose children play with toy guns in Maryland, Democrat state officials across the country are pushing for more gun control laws.

Even Howard Dean, the former Vermont governor and most pro-gun rights supporter among Democratic presidential candidates, wants to renew the so-called semi-automatic assault weapons ban as well as regulate gun shows.

Surprisingly, the Bush administration has basically left most Clinton gun control policies in place. True, Attorney General John Ashcroft decided not to keep long-term records of gun sales and President Bush supports important legislation to curb abusive lawsuits. But the Bush administration has taken few other actions. Clinton administration policies have simply been allowed to continue on everything from existing policies banning the importation of guns to no longer requiring that ROTC military training involve how to fire a gun.

Even when it comes to arming pilots, the administration has twice thwarted congressional legislation. Now over 21 months after September 11, the administration has dragged its feet so that only 44 pilots out of over 100,000 pilots are allowed to carry guns on planes and there are no additional approvals in sight.

In contrast, at the state level Republicans are slowly but steadily rolling back gun regulations. During the last couple of months, concealed handgun laws have been passed in Republican dominated legislatures in Alaska, Colorado, and Minnesota. In Missouri, final passage is uncertain and depends upon whether the Republican dominated legislature can override the Democratic governor's expected veto. The only exception to this Democrat/Republican divide was in New Mexico, which also passed a concealed handgun law this year (albeit an extremely restrictive one), and where Democrats completely control the state legislature and governorship.

Over the last decade, it has been simply impossible to find one study by either the U.S. Justice Department or the Treasury that measures the benefits from people owning guns. For example, every year the Bureau of Alcohol, Tobacco, and Firearms puts out a list of the top 10 guns used in crime, but why not one time put out a list of the top 10 guns used by people to stop crime?

For congressional Democrats, the decision not to push new gun control as a top agenda item is simply because Republicans control both houses of congress. Their strong anti-gun sentiment has not abated. Just two more Democratic senators and 13 more Democratic House members and gun control legislation would go from fond dreams to reality.

Originally appeared June 20, 2003 at FoxNews.com.

Shooting Blanks

This month, the National Academy of Sciences (NAS) issued a 328-page report on gun-control laws.

The big news is that the academy's panel couldn't identify any benefits of the decades-long effort to reduce crime and injury by restricting gun ownership. The only conclusion it could draw was: let's study the question some more (presumably, until we find the results we want).

The academy, however, should believe its own findings. Based on 253 journal articles, 99 books, 43 government publications, a survey that covered 80 different gun-control measures and some of its own empirical work, the panel couldn't identify a single gun-control regulation that reduced violent crime, suicide, or accidents.

From the assault-weapons ban to the Brady Act to one-gun-a-month restrictions to gun locks, nothing worked.

The study was not the work of gun-control opponents: the panel was set up during the Clinton administration, and all but one of its members (whose views on guns were publicly known before their appointments) favored gun control.

It's bad enough that the panel backed away from its own survey and empirical work; worse yet is that it didn't really look objectively at all the evidence. If it had, it would have found not just that gun control doesn't help solve the problems of crime, suicide and gun accidents, but that it may actually be counterproductive.

The panel simply ignored many studies showing just that. For example, the research on gun locks that the panel considered examined only whether accidental gun deaths and suicides were prevented. There was no mention of research that shows that locking up guns prevents people from using them defensively.

The panel also ignored most of the studies that find a correlation between crime reduction and right-to-carry laws. It did pay attention to some non-peer reviewed papers on the right-to-carry issue, and it also noted one part of a right-to-carry study that indicated little or no benefit from such laws. What the panel didn't point out, however, is that the authors of that particular study had concluded that data in their work did much more to show there were benefits than to debunk it.

James Q. Wilson, professor of management and public policy at UCLA, was the one dissenting panelist and the only member whose views were known in advance to not be entirely pro-gun control. His dissent focused on the right-to-carry issue, and the fact that emphasizing results that could not withstand peer-reviewed studies called into question the panel's contention that right-to-carry laws had not for sure had a positive effect.

Wilson also said that that conclusion was inaccurate given that "virtually every reanalysis done by the committee" confirmed right-to-carry laws reduced crime. He found the committee's only results that didn't confirm the drop in crime "quite puzzling." They accounted for "no control variables"—nothing on any of the social, demographic, and public policies that might affect crime—and he didn't understand how evidence that wouldn't get published in a peer-reviewed journal would be given such weight.

While more research is always helpful, the notion that we have learned nothing flies in the face of common sense. The NAS panel should have concluded as the existing research has: gun control doesn't help.

Instead, the panel has left us with two choices: either academia and the government have wasted tens of millions of dollars and countless man-hours on useless research (and the panel would like us to spend more in the same worthless pursuit), or the National Academy is so completely unable to separate politics from its analyses that it simply can't accept the results for what they are.

In either case, the academy—and academics in general—have succeeded mostly in shooting themselves in the foot.

Originally appeared December 29, 2004 in the New York Post.

When It Comes to Firearms, Do as I Say, Not as I Do: Rosie O'Donnell, Who Opposes Handgun Permits for Others, Doesn't See a Problem with Her Bodyguards Having Them

Rosie, say it's not so! The news last week was surprising: Rosie O'Donnell's bodyguards had applied for permits for concealed handguns. Few have declared their opposition to guns as strongly as O'Donnell. For someone who ambushed Tom Selleck on her television show last year on gun control, called for the abolition of the 2nd Amendment and emceed the so-called Million Mom March in Washington, the advice that O'Donnell has freely given others no longer seems to match what she thinks is best for her own family.

Earlier in May on ABCs "This Week," Rosie was asked if she opposed concealed handgun laws. She declared "Of course, I'm against them." She has claimed that "I also think you should not buy a gun anywhere."

O'Donnell previously has been accused of trying to generate attention for her flagging television show by attacking Selleck, despite her agreement with him not to discuss guns. Her credibility was tarnished by appearing in ads for Kmart, a major seller of guns.

Yet the current hypocrisy is more fundamental. A spokeswoman for O'Donnell justifies guns for the talk show host's bodyguards because of threatened violence. But how does her concern differ from what motivates anyone who gets a gun for self-defense? Why does O'Donnell give others advice that she doesn't find applicable to herself?

O'Donnell's response that she still does not "personally own a gun" misses the whole point. Of course, she does not need her own gun when her bodyguards have their guns with them.

Unfortunately, O'Donnell joins a long list of people who demand that others disarm even while they keep their own armed bodyguards. Chicago Mayor Richard Daley, for example, surrounds himself with armed guards even when he visits relatively low-crime areas, but he opposes issuing handgun licenses for people to keep a gun at home in even the most dangerous parts of the city. (Chicago has the highest murder rate of any large city in the U.S.)

For their own safety, people should not follow what O'Donnell preaches, but what she does: get armed protection. As she apparently believes for her own safety, and as the statistics bear out, passive behavior is simply not the wisest course of action. The chance of serious injury from an attack is 2 1/2 times greater for women offering no resistance than for those resisting with a gun. Having a gun is by far the safest course of action, especially for people who are relatively weak physically—women and the elderly.

Concealed handgun permit holders not only protect themselves, but often protect others, though this receives very little media attention. Take the following two incidents occurring the same week as O'Donnell's story hit the media: in Florida, a robber at a Wal-Mart store slashed two employees with a knife, but before he could cause further injuries, 53-year-old Sandra Suter pulled out a pistol and said, "I have a concealed weapons permit. Either drop the knife, or I'll shoot you." After she repeated her threat, the robber dropped his knife.

In Indiana, 70-year-old George Smith stopped two armed robbers at a store because he had a gun. As one of the store clerks saw it, "I think George was the real hero. He saved my life." He likely saved other lives as well, but probably no one outside of Indianapolis has heard of this story. Unfortunately, no one like Suter or Smith was present at Wendy's last week in Brooklyn when five workers were killed. If they had been, and been able to prevent the attack, would that have gotten the same attention? Despite the focus in the media, people use guns defensively about five times more frequently than guns are used to commit crime.

Greenwich, Connecticut, where O'Donnell lives, is one of the wealthiest and safest cities in the United States. Most people there can sleep well at night without a gun for protection. This is not true in many other places, particularly in poorer urban areas. As long as inexpensive guns have not been outlawed, many poor, vulnerable citizens will continue to rely on guns for self-protection.

O'Donnell may be able to afford bodyguards and pride herself on the fact that she does not "personally own a gun." Yet many other people have just as great a need for protection. Guns are the poor man's bodyguard.

Originally appeared June 1, 2000 in the Los Angeles Times, Home Edition.

"The Patriot" is Right

It takes a lot to shock today's jaded movie audiences, especially those at a Hollywood preview. Yet Mel Gibson's new film on the Revolutionary War, "The Patriot," drew loud gasps at a recent screening. The outrageous scene? Gibson's character hands over guns to his 10 and 13-year-old sons to help fight off British soldiers.

Few critics were soothed when the screenwriter noted that the scenes accurately portrayed the complexities of war, or when Gibson said that he would let his own children use guns in self-defense.

With the Clinton administration blaming the recent school violence on the greater accessibility of guns, it is hardly surprising that some are shocked by children using guns. Many people, including George W. Bush and Al Gore, support making it a crime for anyone under the age of 21 to possess a handgun.

Yet gun availability in America has never been as restricted as it is now. As late as 1968, it was possible for children like those in the movie to walk into a hardware store, virtually anywhere in the United States, and buy a rifle. Few states even had age restrictions for buying handguns. Buying a rifle through the mail was easy. Private transfers of guns to juveniles were unrestricted.

But nowhere were guns more common than at school. Until 1969, virtually every public high school in New York City had a shooting club. High-school students carried their guns to school on the subways in the morning, turned them over to their homeroom teacher or the gym coach and retrieved them after school for target practice. The federal government gave club members their rifles and ammunition. Students regularly competed in citywide shooting contests for university scholarships.

Contrast that with what is happening today across the country: college and elementary students are expelled from school for even accidentally bringing a water pistol; elementary school students are suspended for carrying a picture of a gun; kindergarten students are suspended for playing cops and robbers and using their hands as guns; school superintendents lose their jobs for even asking whether someone at a school should have a gun to protect the students. Since the 1960s, the growth of federal gun control has been dramatic. Laws that contained 19,907 words in 1960 quadrupled to 88,413 words by last year. For example, it was not a federal crime for those under 18 to possess a handgun until 1994.

State laws have grown similarly. Even a "gun friendly" state government such as Texas has gun-control provisions of more than 41,000 words. None of this even begins to include the burgeoning local regulations.

But whose access has really been restricted by these laws? While their purpose is obviously to disarm criminals, the laws are primarily obeyed by good people.

There is no academic study showing that waiting periods and background checks have reduced criminal access or resulted in less crime or youth violence. But plenty of research indicates that the reverse is true. The Brady law's waiting periods have delayed access to guns; since its passage, rape rates of women being stalked or threatened have increased.

In Virginia, rural areas have a long tradition of high-school students going hunting in the morning before school. The governor tried in vain to get the state Legislature in 1999 to enact an exemption to the federal "gun-free schools" law in order to let high-school students store their guns in their cars in the school parking lot.

Interestingly, one reason why few students have been prosecuted for possessing a gun on school grounds is that so many offenses involve these very types of cases. Prosecutors find it unreasonable to send good kids to jail simply because they had a rifle locked in the trunk of their car and didn't park sufficiently far enough off of school property. Attempts by Congress to mandate prosecutions will take away this prosecutorial discretion and produce unintended results.

"The Patriot" illustrates the benefits of letting people defend themselves with guns. It is something that has been sorely missing in the current debate. People use guns to stop school shootings or other violent crimes—2 million defensive uses a year. Yet, when was the last time the national evening news carried a story about someone using a gun to save lives?

The horror with which people react to guns is inversely related to how accessible guns are. Whether it was colonial times or 30 years ago, people had more association with guns but less fear. Gun-control advocates face something of a dilemma: if guns are the problem, why was it that when guns were really accessible—even inside schools by students—we didn't have the mass school shootings and other problems that plague us now?

Originally appeared June 22, 2000 in the New York Post.

The Cold, Hard Facts About Guns

America may indeed be obsessed with guns, but much of what passes as fact simply isn't true. The news media's focus only on tragic outcomes, while ignoring tragic events that were avoided, may be responsible for some misimpressions. Horrific events like the recent shooting in Arkansas receive massive news coverage—as they should—but the 2.5 million times each year that people use guns defensively are never discussed—including cases where public shootings are stopped before they happen.

Unfortunately, these misimpressions have real costs for people's safety. Many myths needlessly frighten people and prevent them from defending themselves most effectively.

Myth No. 1: When one is attacked, passive behavior is the safest approach.

The Department of Justice's *National Crime Victimization Survey* reports that the probability of serious injury from an attack is 2.5 times greater for women offering no resistance than for women resisting with a gun. Men also benefit from using a gun, but the benefits are smaller: offering no resistance is 1.4 times more likely to result in serious injury than resisting with a gun.

Myth No. 2: Friends or relatives are the most likely killers.

The myth is usually based on two claims: (1) 58% of murder victims are killed by either relatives or acquaintances and (2) anyone could be a murderer. With the broad definition of "acquaintances" used in the FBI's *Uniform Crime Reports*, most victims are indeed classified as knowing their killer. However, what is not made clear is that acquaintance murder primarily includes drug buyers killing drug pushers, cabdrivers killed by first-time customers, gang members killing other gang members, prostitutes killed by their clients, and so on.

Only one city—Chicago—reports a precise breakdown on the nature of acquaintance killings: between 1990 and 1995 just 17%

of murder victims were family members, friends, neighbors and/or roommates.

Murderers also are not your average citizen. For example, about 90% of adult murderers already have a criminal record as an adult. Murderers are overwhelmingly young males with low IQs and who have difficult times getting along with others. Furthermore, unfortunately, murder is disproportionately committed against blacks and by blacks.

Myth No. 3: The United States has such a high murder rate because Americans own so many guns.

There is no international evidence backing this up. The Swiss, New Zealanders and Finns all own guns as frequently as Americans, yet in 1995 Switzerland had a murder rate 40% lower than Germany's, and New Zealand had one lower than Australia's. Finland and Sweden have very different gun ownership rates, but very similar murder rates. Israel, with a higher gun ownership rate than the U.S., has a murder rate 40% below Canada's. When one studies all countries rather than just a select few as is usually done, there is absolutely no relationship between gun ownership and murder.

Myth No. 4: If law-abiding citizens are allowed to carry concealed handguns, people will end up shooting each other after traffic accidents as well as accidentally shooting police officers.

Millions of people currently hold concealed handgun permits, and some states have issued them for as long as 60 years. Yet, only one permit holder has ever been arrested for using a concealed handgun after a traffic accident and that case was ruled as self-defense. The type of person willing to go through the permitting process is extremely law-abiding.

In Florida, almost 444,000 licenses were granted from 1987 to 1997, but only 84 people have lost their licenses for felonies involving firearms. Most violations that lead to permits being revoked involve accidentally carrying a gun into restricted areas, like airports or schools.

In Virginia, not a single permit holder has committed a violent crime. Similarly encouraging results have been reported for Kentucky, Nevada, North Carolina, South Carolina, Texas and Tennessee (the only other states where information is available).

Myth No. 5: The family gun is more likely to kill you or someone you know than to kill in self-defense.

The studies yielding such numbers never actually inquired as to whose gun was used in the killing. Instead, if a household owned a gun and if a person in that household or someone they knew was shot to death while in the home, the gun in the household was blamed.

In fact, virtually all the killings in these studies were committed by guns brought in by an intruder. No more than 4% of the gun deaths can be attributed to the homeowner's gun. The very fact that most people were killed by intruders also surely raises questions about why they owned guns in the first place and whether they had sufficient protection.

How many attackers have been deterred by the potential victims owning a gun? My own research finds that more concealed handguns, and increased gun ownership generally, unambiguously deter murders, robbery, and aggravated assaults. This is also in line with the well-known fact that criminals prefer attacking victims that they consider weak.

These are only some of the myths about guns and crime that drive the public policy debate. We must not lose sight of the ultimate question: will allowing law-abiding citizens to own guns save lives? The evidence strongly indicates that it does.

Originally appeared May 8, 1998 in the Chicago Tribune,
North Shore Final Edition.

Rampage Killing Facts and Fantasies

The media has a natural inclination to report only dramatic events, preferably those resulting in a dead body, while ignoring potentially tragic events that are avoided. This has created a bad image of gun ownership, for the defensive use of guns—such as preventing murder or theft—is just not newsworthy.

Lately, however, these fears have been further reinforced by an unusual amount of false or misleading statistics from sources like the Clinton administration. The press simply has not been critical enough in questioning the numbers they are given.

However, in a recent case, the press itself now was the source of fraudulent statistics.

In a major 20,000-word series of articles this month on "rampage killings," the *New York Times* declared that its own research "confirmed the public perception that they appear to be increasing." Indeed, the *Times* reported that exactly 100 such attacks took place during the 50 years from 1949 to 1999, with more than half (51) during the five years from 1995 to 1999. With such an apparently huge increase, they concluded "the nation needs tighter gun laws for everyone." Since I have extensively researched mass shootings (together with Professor Bill Landes at the University of Chicago), it was immediately obvious that the Times had simply left out most cases prior to 1995.

The omissions were major; for instance, the *Times* claims that from 1977 to 1995, there was an annual average of only 2.6 attacks where at least one person was killed in a public multiple victim attack (not including robberies or political killings).

Yet our own research uncovered more than 6 times as many cases—an average of 17 per year.

It is only by consistently counting recent cases and ignoring most old ones that the *Times* was able to show that mass killings have been on the increase.

Contrary to their figures, there is no upward national trend at least since the mid-1970s. The data show lots of ups and downs, but with no general rising or falling pattern.

When questioned over the telephone, Ford Fessenden (a

database reporter at the *Times* and the author of the first article in the series) admitted the *Times* staff had concentrated on mainly getting the cases for recent years and that for the early years they only got the "easily obtainable" cases. One hundred simply seemed like a convenient stopping place.

When he asked how long it had taken us to conduct our study, I told him "a couple of thousand hours." His reaction was there was "no way" the *Times* could have devoted that much time to the project. Mr. Fessenden also acknowledged he was familiar with our research and that the article may have given the false impression the *Times* staff was the first to compile this type of data.

The *Times'* claim that attacks increased in the late 1980s and coincided with the time the "production of semiautomatic pistols overtook the production of revolvers" is wrong, for there was no such increase in the late 1980s.

In fact, the opposite was occurring. The number of public shootings per 10 million people fell from 1 in 1985 to .9 in 1990 to .5 in 1995. The *Times'* assertion about pistols makes as much sense as blaming the Brady Law for supposed increase in "rampage killings" during the mid-1990s.

Should "tighter gun laws" be required, as asserted by the *New York Times?* The *Times* staff's conclusion reflects its dismay over the supposed increase in deaths, which they found averaged 33 per year between 1995 and 1999.

Unfortunately, they simply assume tighter gun laws would save lives. However, existing research indicates murder and other crime rates tend to rise with the reforms being advocated.

The proposed rules are particularly useless at stopping these "rampage killings." My research with Mr. Landes examined a range of different policies, including sentencing laws and gun laws (such as waiting periods, background checks, and one-gun-a-month restrictions), to see what might deter these killings. While higher arrest and conviction rates, longer prison sentences, and the death penalty reduce murders generally, neither these measures nor restrictive gun laws had a discernible impact on mass public shootings.

We found only one policy that effectively reduces these attacks:

the passage of right-to-carry laws. But the Times does not even mention this measure.

Giving law-abiding adults the right to carry concealed handguns had a dramatic impact. Thirty-one states now provide such a right under law. When states passed right-to-carry laws, the number of multiple-victim public shootings plummeted below one-fifth, with an even greater decline in deaths. To the extent attacks still occur in states after enactment of these laws, such shootings tend to occur in those areas in which concealed handguns are forbidden. The drop in attacks in states adopting right-to-carry laws has been offset by increases in states without these laws.

The *New York Times* blatantly manipulated its numbers in order to claim a dramatic increase in "rampage killings" and promote a gun-control agenda. There also were other biases in their numbers. Too bad the real world doesn't work the way the *Times* reporters think it should. That is what real research helps us discover.

Originally appeared April 26, 2000 in the Washington Times.

Will Questioning Our Neighbors Make Us Safer?

Should you ask your neighbors if they own a gun?

Recently, a massive advertising and letter-writing campaign tried to persuade parents to do just that. Sponsored by Asking Saves Kids (ASK), an umbrella organization for groups including the National Education Association, the Children's Defense Fund and Physicians for Social Responsibility, the campaign's eye-catching ads pictured a young girl wearing a flak jacket and warned parents against letting their children play in the homes of people who own guns.

ASK's literature tells how to overcome responses such as, "This is not any of your business." Given the risks of young children being "naturally curious," eliminating or locking up guns is explained as just another way of child-proofing a home.

The fear is understandable, but the ASK campaign is still irresponsible. Persuading owners to give up their guns or lock them up out of easy reach will cost more lives than it saves. It also gives a misleading impression of what poses the greatest danger to young children.

Accidental gun deaths among children are fortunately much rarer than most people believe. In 1998, the last year for which the data is available, 53 children younger than 10 years old died from accidental shootings in the United States, about one per state. With some 85 million gun owners and almost 40 million children younger than 10, it is hard to find any item as commonly owned in American homes, as potentially lethal, that has as low an accidental death rate.

These deaths also have little to do with "naturally curious" children shooting other children. No more than five or six of these cases each year involve a child younger than 10 shooting another child.

Overwhelmingly, the shooters are adult males with long histories of alcoholism, arrests for violent crimes, car crashes and suspended or revoked driving licenses. Even if gun locks can stop the few children who abuse a gun from doing so, gun locks cannot stop adults from firing their own guns. It makes a lot more sense to ask your neighbors if they have violent criminal records or histories of substance abuse.

Fear about guns also seems greatest among those who know the least about them. For example, few children possess the strength to cock a pistol or even know how to cock one.

Here are some of the other ways that children younger than 10 died in 1998: Almost 1,100 died as passengers in cars, and cars killed almost another 400 young pedestrians. Bicycle and space-heater accidents take many times more children's lives than guns. Eighty-eight children drowned in bathtubs. Another 36 children younger than age 5 drowned in 5-gallon plastic water buckets.

The real problem with this gun phobia is that without guns, victims are much more vulnerable to criminal attack. Guns are used defensively some 2 million times each year, five times more often than guns are used to commit crimes, according to national surveys from Florida State and Duke Universities, among others. Police are extremely important in reducing crime, but they virtually always arrive after the crime has been committed. Having a gun is by far the safest course of action when confronted by a criminal.

I examined juvenile accidental gun deaths for all states from 1977 to 1996 and found that those states that mandated guns be locked up did not experience a relative drop in accidental deaths. Instead, other problems arose: just as surveys indicated that people were locking up their guns, criminal attacks in people's homes increased and were more successful. The states with these laws had a total increase of 300 more killings and nearly 4,000 more rapes relative to the states without such laws. Burglaries also increased.

States with the largest increases in gun ownership have had the biggest relative drops in violent crime. Each 1% increase in ownership was associated with a 3% drop in violent crime.

Asking neighbors about guns not only strains relationships, it exaggerates dangers and risks lives if neighbors are unarmed when criminals attack. Yet possibly some good can come out of all this gun phobia. If your neighbors ask you whether you own a gun, why not offer to go out to a shooting range together and teach them about guns?

Originally appeared August 29, 2001 in the Hartford Courant.

Armed Response to Shooting
Didn't Really Make the News

Another school shooting occurred last month, and the story was carried everywhere from Australia to Nigeria. This time the shooting occurred at a university, the Appalachian Law School.

As usual, there were calls for more gun control. Yet, in this age of gun-free school zones, one fact was missing from virtually all the news coverage: the attack was stopped by two students who had guns in their cars.

The fast responses of two male students—Mikael Gross, 34, and Tracy Bridges, 25—undoubtedly saved multiple lives. Gross was outside the law school and just returning from lunch when Peter Odighizuwa started his attack. Bridges was in a classroom waiting for class to start.

When the shots rang out, utter chaos erupted. Gross said "People were running everywhere. They were jumping behind cars, running out in front of traffic, trying to get away."

Gross and Bridges did something quite different. Both men immediately ran to their cars and got their guns. Gross had to run about 100 yards to get to his car. Along with Ted Besen (who was unarmed), they approached Odighizuwa from different sides.

As Bridges explained it, "I aimed my gun at him, and Peter tossed his gun down. Ted approached Peter, and Peter hit Ted in the jaw. Ted pushed him back, and we all jumped on."

What is so remarkable is that out of 280 separate news stories (from a computerized Lexis-Nexis search) in the week after the event, just four stories mentioned that the students who stopped the attack had guns. Only two local newspapers (the *Richmond Times-Dispatch* and *The Charlotte Observer*) mentioned that the students actually pointed their guns at the attacker. Much more typical was the scenario described by *The Washington Post*, where the heroes had simply "helped subdue" the killer.

Newsday noted only that the attacker was "restrained by students." Many stories mentioned that the heroic students had law enforcement or military backgrounds, but the media that discussed how the attack was stopped overwhelmingly described it as: "students overpowered a gunman," "students ended the rampage by tackling him," "the gunman was tackled by four male students before being arrested," or "Students ended the rampage by confronting and then tackling the gunman, who dropped his weapon." In all, 72 stories described how the attacker was stopped without mentioning that the student heroes had guns.

Unfortunately, the coverage in this case was not unusual. In the other public school shootings in which citizens with guns have stopped attacks, rarely do more than 1% of the news stories mention that citizens with guns stopped the attacks.

This misreporting actually endangers people's lives. By selectively reporting the news and turning a defensive gun use story into one in which students merely "overpowered a gunman," the media give misleading impressions of what works when people are confronted by violence.

Research consistently shows that having a gun is the safest way to respond to any type of criminal attack, especially these multiple victim shootings.

Originally appeared August 29, 2001 in the Hartford Courant.

Gun Control Misfires in Europe

European gun laws have everything American gun control proponents advocate. Yet, the three worst public shootings in the past year all occurred in Europe. Indeed, around the world, from Australia to England, countries that have recently strengthened gun control laws with the promise of lowering crime have instead seen violent crime soar.

Sixteen people were killed during last Friday's public school shooting in Germany. Compare that to the United States with almost five times as many students, where 32 students and four teachers were killed from any type of gun death at elementary and secondary schools from August 1997 through February 2002, almost five school years. This total includes not only much publicized public school shootings but also gang fights, robberies, and accidents. It all corresponds to an annual rate of one student death per five million students and one teacher death per 4.13 million teachers.

In Europe, shootings have not been limited to schools, of course. The other two worst public shootings were the killing of 14 regional legislators in Zug, a Swiss canton, last September and the massacre of eight city council members in a Paris suburb last month.

So one automatically assumes that European gun laws are easy. Wrong. Germans who wish to get hold of a hunting rifle must undergo background checks that can last one year, while those wanting a gun for sport must be a member of a club and obtain a license from the police. The French must apply for gun permits, which are granted only after an exhaustive background and medical record check and demonstrated need. After all that, permits are only valid for three years.

Even Switzerland's once famously liberal laws have become tighter. In 1999, Switzerland's federation ended policies in half the cantons where concealed handguns were unregulated and allowed to be carried anywhere. Even in many cantons where regulations had previously existed, they had been only relatively liberal. Swiss federal law now severely limits permits only to those who can demonstrate in advance a need for a weapon to protect themselves or others against a precisely specified danger.

All three killing sprees shared one thing in common: they took place in so-called "gun-free safe zones." The attraction of gun-free zone is hardly surprising as guns surely make it easier to kill people, but guns also make it much easier for people to defend themselves. Yet, with "gun-free zones," as with many other gun laws, it is law-abiding citizens, not would-be criminals, who obey them. These laws risk leaving potential victims defenseless.

After a long flirtation with "safe zones," many Americans have learned their lesson the hard way. The U.S. has seen a major change from 1985 when just eight states had liberal right-to-carry laws—laws that automatically grant permits once applicants pass a criminal background check, pay their fees, and, when required, complete a training class. Today the total is 33 states. Deaths and injuries from multiple-victim public shootings, like the three in Europe, fell on average by 78% in states that passed such laws.

The lesson extends more broadly. Violent crime is becoming a major problem in Europe. While many factors, such as law enforcement, drug gangs, and immigration affect crime, the lofty promises of gun controllers can no longer be taken seriously.

In 1996, the U.K. banned handguns. Prior to that time, over 54,000 Britons owned such weapons. The ban is so tight that even shooters training for the Olympics were forced to travel to other countries to practice. In the four years since the ban, gun crimes have risen by an astounding 40%. Dave Rogers, vice chairman of London's Metropolitan Police Federation, said that the ban made little difference to the number of guns in the hands of criminals: "The underground supply of guns does not seem to have dried up at all."

The United Kingdom now leads the United States by a wide margin in robberies and aggravated assaults. Although murder and rape rates are still higher in the United States, the difference is shrinking quickly.

Of course, advocates of gun control look for ways to get around any evidence. Publications such as the *New York Times* and the *Los Angeles Times* blame Europe's increasing crime problems on a seemingly unstoppable black market that "has undercut . . . strict gun-control laws." Let's say that's the case. Even then, these gun laws clearly did not deliver the promised reductions in crime.

It is hard to think of a much more draconian police state than the former Soviet Union, yet despite a ban on guns that dates back to the communist revolution, newly released data suggest that the "worker's paradise" was less than the idyllic picture painted by the regime in yet another respect: murder rates were high. During the entire decade from 1976 to 1985 the Soviet Union's homicide rate was between 21% and 41% higher than that of the United States. By 1989, two years before the collapse of the Soviet Union, it had risen to 48% above U.S. rate.

In fact, the countries with by far the highest homicide rates have gun bans.

Originally appeared April 30, 2002 in the Wall Street Journal Europe.

PART TWO

Other Freedoms, Studies and Musings

PART TWO

Bogus Discrimination Claims

with Stephen G. Brounars

The NBA has the best record in professional sports in hiring black coaches. But the *New York Times* got that record wrong late last March in a 2,200-word front-page story.

The *Times'* study of the past 15 years found evidence of discrimination against black coaches. A white coach, the paper claimed, typically gets to coach "50 percent longer [than a black coach] and has most of an extra season to prove himself." Discrimination is abhorrent, and the *Times'* evidence of discrimination caused real, understandable anger in sports pages across the nation.

But there are serious problems with the evidence. For starters, the *Times* authors, David Leonhardt and Ford Fessenden, selectively threw out data (such as not looking at current coaches). In fact, in one difficult-to-understand sentence buried deep in the article, they admit that if these data are included, "the gap between white and black coaches was nearly identical." Yet they offered no explanation for why they threw that data out.

And even with selective use of data, the differences they found are not statistically significant. In other words, their "evidence" doesn't show anything.

As Harvard Professor Larry Katz, an expert that the *Times* consulted, noted to us, the best research on this topic (by Larry Kahn at Cornell University) "finds no significant race differences" between black and white NBA coaches using "almost any reasonable set of controls." Yet the *Times* made no mention of any opposing evidence. The *Times* refuses to share the data used in its published stories, making it more difficult for others to analyze and criticize the newspaper's statistical study in a timely fashion.

The *Times* reported that from 1990 to 2004, black coaches lasted an average of 1.6 seasons, while white coaches kept their jobs for an average of 2.4 seasons. The study excluded coaches who had served more than 10 years, coaches who had coached any time prior to 1990 and active coaches. Using data that we gathered independently with the same rules outlined by the *Times*, we found that black coaches lasted for 1.7 seasons compared to 2.57 seasons for white coaches. More than a third of the coaches were black, with all but two teams having employed at least one black coach.

But any empirical work explaining a coach's length of service should account for things like a coach's win rate and experience, among other factors.

In particular, a proper study must also note general changes in coaching durations over time. Coaching tenures are getting ever shorter even as black coaches have become more common; ignoring these trends would lead to a spurious correlation between race and coaching length of service.

Though we looked at a data set similar to what the *Times* said it selected, it seems most appropriate to concentrate on all the coaches serving after 1990, even those still coaching. It turns out that—contrary to the *Times'* study—white and black coaches have similar lengths of service.

Winning substantially helps job security (each one percentage-point increase in the win rate increases a coach's job duration by at least 8%)—and it seems to help white and black coaches equally. But for some reason, if all else is equal, NBA teams win more often with a white coach—teams with white coaches had an eighth percentage-point higher win rates. (That is, a .08 difference in the three-digit "winning percentage" seen on most sports pages.)

The *Times* article focuses on anecdotal evidence supporting its contention that black coaches face discrimination, but there are at least as many examples to demonstrate that black coaches in the NBA are treated fairly. For example, Doc Rivers lasted over 4 seasons in Orlando even though his win rate (.504) was less than the win rate for the three previous white coaches who averaged just 1.9 seasons of service.

Even Paul Silas, the black coach that the *Times* notes was treated poorly in Cleveland, spent 4.4 years with the Charlotte/New Orleans Hornets, as compared to Dave Cowens' 2.1 years—even though his .573 win rate was lower than Cowens' .609 win rate.

Mr. Leonhardt suggests that concerns about issues such as selectively dropping data and statistical significance aren't really relevant because the *Times* is "not an academic journal, it is a newspaper." Yet the fact remains that the *Times*—a newspaper with millions of readers—alleges discrimination on the basis of evidence that simply doesn't hold up. That's the equivalent of yelling "fire" in a crowded movie theater.

Originally appeared May 12, 2005 in the Washington Times.

Affirmative Action Has Mixed Results for Cops

In the furor that followed a daring and allegedly deadly Atlanta courthouse escape on March 11, 2005, some pointed to the differences in strength and size of the suspect and the female deputy guarding him as a key factor that allowed the man to get a gun.

But what has been ignored in the case of Brian Nichols is the role that affirmative action has played in hiring standards for police.

There are extremely important benefits to having police departments that mirror the characteristics of the general population. Females and minorities are important for undercover work. A female victim of crime might feel more comfortable talking to another woman. Women might be particularly useful in domestic violence cases.

The same holds true for minority victims of crime. Minority officers who come from the local communities they are policing might also bring knowledge about the area that makes them more effective officers.

The problem is that because of large differences in strength and size between men and women, different standards are applied to ensure that there are more female officers. In the Nichols case, the difference was stark: the suspect was 33 years old and 6 feet tall; the female sheriff's deputy guarding him was 51 years old and 5-foot-2.

Similarly, the intelligence tests used to screen officers have produced different pass rates for different racial groups. To eliminate those differences, there has been a strong move to stop giving these tests over the last 30 years.

Some argue that these criteria were not important in picking officers, or that intelligence tests are culturally biased—or worse, that the screening criteria exist primarily to ensure that women and minorities are excluded from the profession. There is possibly some truth to this, but there is still the question about how far one goes to ensure that a police force mirrors the community it is protecting.

Some of these differences are fairly large. For example, in a study I published in 2000 examining the effect of affirmative action on police hiring, a comparison of male and female public safety officers found that female officers had 32 to 56% less upper-body strength and

18 to 45% less lower-body strength than male officers.

In New York City, because the physical strength rules were so weakened during the 1980s, a former NYPD personnel chief complained at one time that many police officers "lack the strength to pull the trigger on a gun" and do not have the physical strength to run after suspects.

Part of these differences between men and women can be offset by changing technology and operating procedures. Cars can replace foot and bicycle patrols. Two-officer units can replace single-officer units, though these changes mean less contact between officers and the public and less area covered.

Officers can also be issued more protective gear. Indeed, my own published research finds these exact changes in police departments when hiring standards are changed for women.

We also see that as a greater percentage of a department is made up of women, the competition among men for the remaining slots increases and the average strength and size of men admitted actually rises, partly offsetting the weaker strength of the newer female officers.

The net effect of changing hiring rules for women is mixed. I couldn't find any significant overall change in crime rates when more female police officers were hired (though rape rates did decline). There were some less desirable consequences, and they fit in with the recent experience we have just seen in the Atlanta courthouse attack.

Increasing the number of women officers under these reduced strength and size standards consistently and significantly increases the number of assaults on police officers. In general, every 1% increase in the number of women in a police force results in a 15 to 19% increase in the number of assaults on the police, because women tend to be weaker than men.

Why? The more likely that a criminal's assault on a police officer will be successful, the more likely criminals will do it. The major factor determining success is the relative strengths and sizes of the criminal and officer. The 200-pound Nichols might have decided not to try to escape had his guard been closer to his own size.

My research uncovered another interesting finding. Female

officers are more likely to accidentally shoot people. Each 1% increase in the number of white female officers in a police force increases the number of shootings of civilians by 2.7%. Because of their weaker physical strength, female officers have less time to decide on whether to fire their weapon. If a man makes a mistake and waits too long to shoot a suspect who is attacking him, the male officer still has a chance of using his strength to subdue the attacker. Female officers (as was the case in Atlanta) will lose control of the situation at that point.

While creating a more diverse police force may produce some benefits, we still shouldn't forget the differences between men and women. Just as women officers are better suited for some jobs, there are other jobs that simply call for large men.

Originally appeared March 28, 2005 at FoxNews.com.

An Organization Pregnant with Contradictions

with April Dabney

Women's bodies are theirs to do what they want, but for the National Organization for Women (NOW) that only seems true as long as what the women want to do is politically correct. Despite NOW's rhetoric, the laws they have come out supporting the last couple of weeks appear to have more to do with forcing women to live the way NOW wants them to live then letting women have the freedom to make these decisions themselves.

In the last couple of weeks NOW has launched several campaigns, among them:

• Some pharmacists have moral objections to selling the so-called "morning after pill." Even though there are virtually always other nearby pharmacists and that any chain store with such a pharmacist makes arrangements for someone else to fulfill the prescription, NOW believes that even that small inconvenience places too great of a burden on a woman's right to use her body as she sees fit, and thus such practices should be outlawed.

• NOW is also fighting for a continued ban on silicone breast implants. They claim that the claimed health risks are just too great for women to be given the choice of using these implants.

Health concerns have been raised for both the pill and implants, but health concerns aren't really the problem here. Few products have been studied as extensively as breast implants. A Food and Drug Administration (FDA) panel recently approved the use of some silicone breast implants, and silicone is used in numerous other medical devices. Comprehensive analyses from the UK Independent Review Panel on Silicone Gel Breast Implants (1998), the Institute of Medicine (1999), and the National Cancer Institute (2004) as well as journal publications such as Plastic and Reconstructive Surgery (2004) have consistently found no health problems. Even when implants have ruptured, concerns about immunological or connective tissue diseases or cancers simply haven't been born out by the research.

In addition, NOW is still fighting the last war by pointing to anecdotal stories of problems the implants used during the 1970s and 1980s even though the technology has vastly improved since then. It is hard to see why anyone would think that the newer third and fourth generation implants, which have been used outside the U.S. since 1995, pose any risk. Unlike the earlier implants where the silicone was runny and had the consistency of motor oil, the newer substances are jellylike or have an even more stable consistency. With the fourth generation, rupture simply isn't relevant because the silicone won't spread.

There are also other benefits. The type of woman who gets breast implants tends to have high rates of suicide, but as Joseph McLaughlin, Ph.D., of the International Epidemiology Institute in Maryland notes, that it is seems that "without the implants, the suicide rate would be even higher." Most women who get the implants generally indicate that they are happier than they were prior to getting them.

Because of deaths from women taking the morning after pill, the FDA has ordered its highest-level warning placed on packages, but even there the risks of death are quite small (a total of five deaths in the US have been linked to the pill, though it was announced this week that more deaths are being investigated). The anecdotal deaths from this pill are much more tightly linked to the pill than is true for the anecdotal stories of problems from the implants, but NOW has never questioned making the pill as widely available to women as possible (even for young underage girls).

The costs and benefits to a woman from pregnancy seem much bigger than those from an implant, but that doesn't explain why we trust the judgment of a thirteen year old in deciding whether to take the morning after pill but not a twenty-five-year-old who wants implants. There appears to be a general theme connecting NOW's positions that make it easier for women of all ages to avoid having kids and discourage them from trying to attract men.

One can even sympathize with NOW's argument that women shouldn't have to feel that they must go under the knife to be attractive. But women have no unique corner on this burden. News anchors get facelifts and politicians take Botox. Wall Street traders take Ritalin and everyone uses caffeinated drinks during work to stay alert and be more successful. Professional athletes sometimes undergo extensive surgeries to keep playing their sports.

If it makes television news viewers happier to watch a more youthful news anchor by more than the cost and discomfort from the surgery, what is so wrong with news anchors voluntarily getting the procedure? Would the country really be better off if we all didn't strive so hard to be the best at what we do?

Ironically, the same organization that says that a woman rights to make the decisions that affect her body when it comes to abortion are sacrosanct, says those same rights are irrelevant when the woman wants to put something in her body to make herself look and feel better. Possibly if NOW members were more confident of their arguments, they wouldn't feel it as necessary to mandate what women can and can't do.

Originally appeared August 16, 2005, at Tech Central Station.

Unserious Suggestions:
Silly Democratic Consultations

with Sonya D. Jones

Senate Democrats implore President Bush to consult with them and they have not ruled out the prospect of filibustering a nominee they consider too extreme. Commentators such as Gloria Borger go on to claim that "real consultation [over a Supreme Court nominee]... is about honest exchanges with key Democrats to ensure the public gets what it wants..."

Last week, Bush was clearly consulting with the Senate over breakfast with Democrats Harry Reid and Pat Leahy as well as Republicans Arlen Specter and Bill Frist. While the press portrays Democrats as being cooperative by offering Bush the names of conservatives who they regard as reasonable and who would meet with their approval, their suggestions were less serious than first meets the eye.

Democrats suggested the names of three sitting judges: Ricardo Hinojosa, Edward Prado, and Sonia Sotomayor. The problem is that in the same breath that the Democrats acknowledge that Bush will appoint a conservative, the Democratic senators may be only ones that might view their suggestions as conservative. The contrast in the helpful advice that Orrin Hatch offered President Clinton in 1993 could not be more stark.

Hatch's criteria were simple. He suggested liberals who "were highly honest and capable jurists and their confirmation would not embarrass the president."

Few would deny that either Ruth Bader Ginsberg or Stephen Breyer was a strong liberal. Prior to their nominations, Breyer served as Senator Ted Kennedy's special counsel to the Senate Judiciary Committee and Ginsberg was the general counsel for the American Civil Liberties Union. Their voting records on the Court have only confirmed those beliefs. On issues such as the constitutionality of the death penalty for minors, reliance on foreign law and constitutions for interpreting our own constitution, whether the government can take someone's property to give to another private party, how the federal government can regulate essentially everything, or abortion, Breyer and Ginsberg have taken consistently liberal positions.

Hatch also didn't shrink away from suggesting nominees from intellectual heavyweights who could alter the direction of the court. Breyer, a professor at the Harvard Law School, had written widely on regulatory issues. Both Breyer and Ginsburg had been published widely in academic journals, books, and more popular publications. Hatch suggested nominees whom Clinton would regard as strong choices.

While Republicans might accidentally end up with a liberal justice such as John Paul Stevens or David Souter, it is pretty safe to say that a Republican president wouldn't nominate the general counsel for the ACLU to the nation's highest court.

Yet, take the Democrats suggestions for Bush. For example, Judge Sonia Sotomayor was a Clinton nominee to the circuit court. Do Democrats really think that Bush would pick a Clinton nominee? How would Clinton and Democrats have reacted if Hatch has suggested he nominate either a Reagan or Bush 41 circuit-court judge to the Supreme Court?

What is more amazing though is how the media has portrayed this process. Only about a sixth of the news stories on Sotomayor even mention her appointment by Clinton.

Another measure is provided by The Almanac of the Federal Judiciary, which surveys courtroom lawyers on the political views of the judges they encounter in their litigation. The survey asks lawyers whether the judge is "liberal," "moderate," "conservative," "libertarian," or "neutral." Given that these are lawyers (a fairly liberal group being surveyed), it is possible what they view as "moderate" might be considered "liberal" to most other Americans. The survey rates Sotomayor as either a "moderate" or "neutral "politically and Ricardo Hinojosa as a "moderate"—no lawyer who argued before them considered either one "conservative." Only Edward Prado is viewed by any of the practicing lawyers as "conservative," and views of him are evenly split between being "conservative" and "neutral."

Nor do the Democrats have much to worry about any of their suggestions being very influential on the Court. Unlike the names offered by Hatch, none of the Democratic suggestions have previously distinguished themselves in past writings. Indeed, none have published a journal article, book, or even an article in a newspaper or magazine.

Given recent statements by Senator Chuck Schumer that indicate the Democrats are plotting to stymie any possible Bush nominee, it is somewhat hard to take Democratic demands seriously. It may have been a dream to think that Democrats would show Bush the same courtesy that Hatch showed Clinton.

Originally appeared July 17, 2005 at National Review Online.

High on Hype: Congress "Takes On" Steroids

with Sonya D. Jones

Politicians simply cannot leave well enough alone. Even a Republican Congress seems unable to resist the lure of publicity and accept that private companies might do a better job than itself of figuring out what customers want.

Last year, it was Senator John McCain (R., Arizona) who threatened baseball with government-imposed standards unless the sport adopted rules that he thought was acceptable. Today, in a move more reminiscent of Congresses long ago subpoenaing the Mafia, the House Government Reform Committee will try forcing seven baseball players to testify before their committee. Last Sunday, congressmen appeared on national television threatening the players with jail sentences if they didn't buckle under. They threatened the league with losing its antitrust and tax exemptions.

Baseball responded after the first threats, adopting year-round testing of players and more severe penalties. But despite the blessing of McCain, the changes haven't apparently satisfied everyone in Congress.

The committee's chairman, Representative Tom Davis (R., Virginia) dismisses baseball's new rules, justifying the tough threats because steroid use by juveniles "is a public health crisis. [W]e have the parents of kids who have used steroids and committed suicide."

The *New York Times* ran a long story this month on a high-school-student, Efrain Marrero, whose family claims that his stopping using steroids provides a "plausible explanation" for his suicide. While there is no scientific evidence linking steroids and suicide, the Times points to "persuasive anecdotal evidence."

Yet, some perspective is needed here. While Davis claims that currently "over a half a million youth are using steroids," the Times notes that, in addition to Marrero, only "two previous suicides had been attributed by parents to steroid use by young athletes." With steroid use in high schools dating back to the 1950s, the suicide rate—even if Marrero's death were actually linked to steroids and not other factors—seems negligible compared to a male suicide rate for 15-to-24-year-olds, which has averaged more than 20 per 100,000 over the last 30 years.

Even more startling is how the young male suicide rate has fallen over the last decade while steroid use has grown. On Meet the Press, Representative Henry Waxman (D., California) claimed that over the last decade, steroid use had risen from one out of every 45 kids to one out of 16, while the young male suicide rate has gone down from 26 to 20 per 100,000.

To lose one's child seems unimaginable, and the desire to explain it is understandable. Perhaps the parents are right in these cases, but congressional hearings should focus on the real risks endangering children's lives. Considering that 397 teenagers die per year from drowning, 77 from bicycling, 504 from poisonings, and 91 from just simple falls, it is difficult to understand the hysteria over steroids.

The risks seem pretty mild for professional players. Last spring, a baseball players' union representative, Gene Orza, claimed that steroids are "not worse than cigarettes." With over 4,000 people playing major-league baseball over the last decade and claims that 40 to 50% of players are using some form of anabolic steroids, what is striking is how rare baseball deaths are and that these are not really related to "performance-enhancing" drugs. Take the last two years:

• In October 2004, 41-year-old retired baseball star Ken Caminiti's death from a heart attack caused a stir — but it proved a false alarm. The medical examiner ruled that the death was due to an overdose of cocaine and opiates.

• In 2003, the Baltimore Orioles's Steve Bechler died during spring training while taking a diet aid, ephedra (a stimulant). Sen. Dick Durbin (D., Illinois) quickly rushed forward with legislation to require stricter standards. It only became clear later that the death likely had another cause: Bechler had a history of heart problems, came to camp out of shape and way overweight, and was playing while dehydrated and not eating.

Scott Gottlieb, a former senior policy adviser to the commissioner of the Food and Drug Administration, notes: "There are plenty of people with [multiple sclerosis], Crohn's and colitis, and rheumatoid arthritis and lupus and other diseases, who are on much higher doses of chronic steroids. Certainly, they have a lot of side effects, but they don't drop dead of [heart attacks] so easily."

With Congress grossly exaggerating the "public health crisis" from suicides to justify their involvement, it is hard to believe that their motives are based on little more than grabbing attention. Congress has already intervened too much with threats and ought to leave baseball alone and let them work out their own problems. Baseball has already made changes, but those changes have not been given any time to see if they work. If this is a continuing problem, the fans will speak loudly and clearly, letting a private company know exactly what the customer wants.

Originally appeared March 17, 2005, at National Review Online.

The Felon Vote

with James K. Glassman

In the wake of their election defeat, Democrats have promised to mend their ways by emphasizing moral values. So, in their first major legislative initiative of the year, what are the party's two top senators offering? A bill to guarantee that millions of convicted murderers, rapists, armed robbers, and those who have violently assaulted others can vote.

This week, Senators Hillary Rodham Clinton and John Kerry will officially introduce the Count Every Vote Act, which she claims is "critical to restoring America's faith in our voting system." Among the provisions: A measure to insure that voting rights are restored to "felons who have repaid their debt to society" by completing their prison terms, parole or probation.

Senator Clinton says there are 4.7 million such disenfranchised felons in 48 states and the District of Columbia.

The power to deny voting rights to ex-convicts now rests with the states, so standards vary across the country. The 14th Amendment to the Constitution explicitly allows for states to deny felons the right to vote.

Clinton and Kerry do have good reason to want ex-convicts to vote: felons overwhelmingly vote for Democrats.

In recent academic work, Jeff Manza and Marcus Britton of Northwestern University and Christopher Uggen of the University of Minnesota estimated that Bill Clinton pulled 86% of the felon vote in 1992 and a whopping 93% in 1996.

The researchers found that about 30% of felons vote when given the chance. So, if all 4.7 million of Mrs. Clinton's ex-cons are re-enfranchised, about 1.4 million will cast ballots, and about 1.2 million of those will be for Democrats.

Manza & Co.'s results indicate that this "felon vote" would have given Democrats the White House in the 2000 and control of the Senate from 1986 to 2004.

Seattle Times reporters last month identified 129 felons in

King and Pierce counties who had voted illegally in the November 2nd election—in a race that Democrat Christine Gregoire won by—coincidentally—129 votes. Extrapolating the illegal felon vote across the entire state, one can conclude that Gregoire owes her controversial victory to ex-cons who should not have voted—but did.

Why shouldn't felons be able to vote if they have paid their debt to society? Simply because society believes that the debt includes a prohibition on voting.

It is hardly a radical notion to penalize felons long after they have left prison or completed parole. Laws deny ex-cons the right to hold office, to retain professional licenses (lawyers, for example, lose their ability to practice), or to serve as an officer in a publicly traded company. Felons, by law, can in some cases lose their right to inherit property, to collect pension benefits or even to get a truck-driving license.

In fact, in most states, the loss of voting rights does not last as long as other prohibitions.

Looked at from the punishment angle, it is no more obvious why all states should impose the same rules on felons voting than why they should have the same prison terms or why they should impose all these other penalties for the same length of time.

In addition, post-sentence penalties are placed on criminals not only who have committed felonies but who have committed misdemeanors, including, under federal law, the right to own a gun. We doubt that Clinton and Kerry will be crusading to restore that right any time soon.

When people harm others, we learn something about them. Do we want someone who has committed multiple rapes helping determine how much money will be spent on social programs that help rape victims?

Clinton and Kerry appear to be angling, not for the votes of centrists but for the votes of the most dedicated left-wing constituency in America: criminals. We doubt, however, that most Americans believe that felons comprise a minority group that deserves such special favors.

Originally appeared March 1, 2005, in the New York Post

Social Security Reform Won't Boost U.S. Debt

with Robert G. Hansen

The Social Security debate is quickly becoming one of how to finance any reforms. On Wednesday, the President stated that he was open to raising Social Security taxes and Alan Greenspan, while voicing some support for private retirement accounts, also raised concern about effects on capital markets of aggressive transition to privatizing social security.

Forty-four Democratic US Senators have signed a letter ruling out any new debt.

Yet, the whole debate is wrong headed. Social security privatization need not have any impact on net debt for our economy or for the government.

Senators such as Richard Durbin (D., Illinois) charge that the reforms will add "2 trillion to $5 trillion addition to America's national debt" and reporters constantly ask, "how are you going to pay for that?"

This debate rests on an accounting fiction that fails to recognize the government's real liabilities as current debt.

Take an example where people can invest $100 of current social security contributions into individual retirement accounts rather than the social security fund and in return future social security benefits are cut by the equivalent of $100 today.

The loss of $100 in current taxes requires an additional $100 of debt to be issued, but the government's obligatory future social security benefits are reduced.

MUCH OBLIGED

Why should we treat future social security obligations as less real than obligations to pay future interest and principal payments?

Surely no politician will argue that the former are less likely to occur and should therefore not be recognized as real obligations.

As another way to see how real the government's future

obligations on social security are, there is a very simple way for the government to create personal retirement accounts without raising any additional debt.

All the government has to do is allow individuals to sell some portion of their future social security benefits in exchange for a lump sum payment today.

Wall Street makes these present value and life expectancy calculations all the time for annuities. Individuals who receive the lump sum payments would turn around and invest the money in diversified funds approved by the government and that would hold some mixture of stocks and bonds.

The entire round trip is a net wash: banks raise money by selling debt that is backed by current social security promises, but individuals immediately return the same amount back to the capital markets.

The net drain on capital markets is zero.

There are real advantages to creating private retirement accounts in this way. Individuals would receive a lump sum that they could invest in assets appropriate for their time horizon and risk preferences, rather than being forced to accept the government's (low but riskless) rate of return inherent in social security as it stands.

Rough calculations suggest that if we allowed a 45 year-old person to capitalize one-third of their expected social security benefits, they would get about $50,000 today. A personal retirement account funded to that level puts real meaning to the term ownership society.

CUTTING DEBT

President Bush's proposal though actually reduces government debt. By voluntarily joining the program and getting the benefits of the higher returns and keeping the money, participants must agree to a reduction in future benefits that is slightly larger than the current reduction in taxes.

Unfortunately, this is all being missed in the debate. A computerized search of news stories over the last week finds over a thousand news stories mischaracterizing the reforms as causing us to go further into debt. Imagine the outcry among the press if private companies used the government's accounting rules. Firms could reduce worker's wages today in exchange for larger pension and health care benefits in the future.

Those future pension benefits that are paid more than 10 years in the future would not appear on the balance sheet, but the cut in current wages would increase reported profits. Of course, no one would believe the claimed "profits." Similarly, no one should believe the claims of government "debt."

An honest debate can be had over whether we continue with a pay-as-you-go, defined benefits system, where retirement funds are never invested, or a defined contribution retirement program that allows individuals to tap into the power of tax free compound returns.

Undoubtedly, much of this is the fault of bizarre Federal accounting rules, but it is not clear how we can have a real debate with all these accounting fictions.

Counting only current changes in revenue and not future changes in liability would land people in jail if they were working for anyone other than the government.

Originally appeared February 28, 2005 in Investors' Business Daily.

Eliminating Sentencing Guidelines
Would Make Penalties More Equal

By a 5-4 margin, the Supreme Court effectively put the *U.S. Sentencing Commission Guidelines* out of their misery in January. The *Guidelines* were originally set up in 1987 to ensure fairness and rational organization in criminal sentencing. But they have failed, instead increasing disparities and making an illogical hodgepodge of rules.

Critics of the *Guidelines* have focused on its many eccentricities. For instance, penalties for drug violations are based upon the weight rather than the purity of the drugs (note to would-be criminals: to minimize jail, make sure the cocaine is pure and not diluted with baking soda or sugar).

Yet, a more basic problem exists. The *Guidelines* have created more sentencing disparity because they focus solely on just one of the penalties that criminals face: imprisonment. There are many other penalties imposed on criminals, including lost professional and business licenses, the inability to join some unions or work for the government, lost retirement funds as well as fines and restitution. Prior to the *Guidelines* going into effect, judges usually imposed lower prison sentences on criminals who faced large other additional penalties.

Martha Stewart's recent case is a good example of the inequities created by the guidelines. She was sentenced to 10 months confinement, but she also suffered millions of dollars in lost salary, lower stock market value of her company, and fines. A common criminal who was similarly convicted of misleading authorities would only face the prison term. In the absence of the guidelines, Martha Stewart's prison sentence would have been shorter and her case become one of those "disparities" that people used to complain about twenty years ago.

True sentencing disparities for the same crime that motivated the *Guidelines* were actually rare. A false impression usually arising simply from a failure to recognize that most judges prior to the *Guidelines* were balancing all the penalties born by the criminals.

For many first time criminals, these additional penalties are more important than the imprisonment itself. To illustrate their importance, in the mid-1980s, the average insider trader made $365,000 per year in legitimate earnings prior to conviction, but only $14,000 per year during the last year on probation or parole. Only a few percent of these people faced prison and those terms were just a couple of months long. While this example is extreme, not just white-collar criminals face substantial cuts in income. Even the typical larcenist, who faced about 4 months in jail, faced a reduction from $15,000 prior to conviction down to $10,000.

The dissents by Justices Anthony Scalia and Clarence Thomas were right in that all the *Guidelines* don't have to be thrown out just because a small section of the *Guidelines* that applied to some trials violated Constitutional rights to a jury trial. Yet, the jabs Scalia pokes at the majority's seeming inability to grasp the inconsistency between making the *Guidelines* voluntary and saving their mission to reduce sentencing disparity missed a crucial point. The critique only makes sense if the *Guidelines* actually reduced disparity.

In part, Scalia's assumptions about how the *Guidelines* work arise because, according to him, "the *Guidelines* took pre-existing sentencing practices into account." But, unfortunately, as people who worked there know, only a small part of the *Guidelines* had anything to do with past practice and even that was quickly done away with. Many crimes, such as insider trading, faced explicit prohibitions within the commission against collecting any data on past sentences.

For bank larceny (the only category where *Guidelines* were originally based on past practice), the revised 1989 guidelines, issued just two years after the initial ones, eliminated any real link to past practice. In order to increase penalties half the data sample was dropped – the cases with the lowest prison terms. For other crimes the sentences were based at best on guesses of what constituted past practice.

With a new battle to reform sentencing brewing in congress after the court's decision, hopefully congress will heed an earlier description by Scalia of the commission as "a sort of junior-varsity Congress," that contained all the political weaknesses with out the constraints. Indeed, as the news media has focused on new stories over the years, the *Guidelines* have responded and become an ever more complicated patchwork quilt of often-inconsistent rules.

The *Guidelines* overturned many sensible patterns of imposing legal penalties, patterns that had arisen over decades. For example, in the past, secretly dumping a small amount of oil illegally into water received a much higher penalty relative to the damage done compared to a major oil tanker running a ground. From an economic point of view, this makes perfect sense, as crimes that are difficult to detect must be punished more severely. The *Guidelines* reversed these and other long time patterns.

The court's decision, unfortunately, may only provide a temporary respite. Hopefully though, instead of merely keep on repeating the need for fair sentencing, the new legislative push will actually adopt a system that doesn't again do the opposite.

Originally appeared February 7, 2005 in Investors' Business Daily.

Exploding the Fireworks Safety 'Threat'

As Americans celebrate their freedom on Sunday, it will be with a certain irony: not all Americans have the freedom to celebrate the holiday with the traditional festive bang. Though about 70 million of us live in states that allow all sorts of fireworks and firecracker use, 50 million other Americans who live in nine states, including New York and Arkansas, need a permit to even light a sparkler. The state of California bans some types of fireworks and allows cities to expand what is prohibited. Safety is the major concern of those who ban our celebratory backyard light and noise shows, but their fears are overblown.

In fact, banning personal use of fireworks may actually result in more accidental fires because some of those who try to avoid getting caught set them off in remote fields, causing fires that take longer to discover.

This issue is badly distorted by the media. A search of the top 100 newspapers found 140 news stories in the last year warning that fireworks could be deadly if used improperly. But despite this edge to the coverage, on average just six people a year died in fireworks-related incidents from 1990 to 2002. And many of those deaths occurred at professional fireworks displays.

By comparison, about 20 times more children under the age of 10 drown in home bathtubs each year than the number of people who are killed in fireworks accidents. Despite the fears raised by the media, fireworks deaths are just not something that people should spend any time worrying about.

It is hard to see much of a relationship over the years between fireworks use and deaths. Though almost exactly the same number of people died in 1990 and 2002, fireworks use grew almost every year, soaring from 68 million pounds of explosives used to 221 million pounds.

States such as New Jersey that have adopted more stringent regulations or bans haven't seen significant drops in the number of fireworks-related deaths, in part because there were few such deaths to begin with. During the last three years, states with bans actually had a higher fireworks-related death rate (.018 per million people) than the states without restrictions (.014 per million).

Injuries are much more difficult to track, but there were an estimated 8,700 fireworks-related injuries treated in hospital emergency rooms during 2002, the vast majority relatively trivial. This is only a fraction of the 208,000 injuries suffered in bathtubs from falls, scalding water and even electrocution.

The simple volume of the explosives sold across the United States raises a question: how effective can any ban possibly be, short of erecting a wall around a state?

In Los Angeles, a city that Mayor James K. Hahn claims has "zero tolerance for fireworks," a man was arrested last week for storing 15 tons of illegal fireworks in different parts of the city. Given how close this is to the Fourth of July, who knows how many fireworks he had already distributed?

Educating the public about how to safely use fireworks is preferable to bans. Such education is not just about where and how to set off the explosions. William Weimer, vice president of Phantom Fireworks, recently made a pretty simple point: a lot of the accidents result from people drinking too much alcohol. As he put it, "If you've been drinking, you should have a designated igniter, just like you should have a designated driver."

Government can protect people from only so much, and if we banned all the products that caused more deaths and injuries than fireworks, there would be virtually nothing left to use. After all, what is the Fourth of July celebrating if we criminalize even the tiny risks associated with fireworks?

Originally appeared June 30, 2004 in the Los Angeles Times.

Moore's Myths

with Brian Blasé

Among its many errors, Michael Moore's "Fahrenheit 9/11" is poisoning our political debate with its fictional account of the Florida vote in 2000.

Perhaps his distortions have gone without remark because they've been repeated so often. (Jesse Jackson, for one, still speaks of Florida as "the scene of the crime" where "[blacks] were disenfranchised. Our birthright stolen.") But still, Moore's "documentary" seems to set a new record for political dishonesty.

Consider a few of the movie's assertions:

• The Fox News Channel played a major role in Bush's victory in Florida: The film shows CBS and CNN calling Florida for Gore, followed by a voice-over uttering, "Then something called the Fox News Channel called the election in favor of the other guy."

• First off, Moore leaves out the fact that Fox first called Florida for Gore—and didn't call it back until 2 a.m.

• Indeed, all the networks, Fox included, helped Gore by calling the Florida polls as closed at 7 p.m. Eastern time — and quickly declaring a Democrat the winner of the state's U.S. Senate race, before also saying the state had gone to Gore.

• In fact, polls in the 10 heavily Republican counties in the state's western panhandle, located in the Central time zone, were open until 8. But why bother trying to vote when a trusted newsman says the polls are closed and you've already lost?

• After surveying voters, Democratic strategist Bob Beckel claimed that the early call cost Bush a net loss of up to 8,000 votes. Another survey conducted by John McLaughlin and Associates, a Republican polling company, put Bush's net loss at about 10,000 votes.

• "Under every scenario Gore would have won" the Florida vote if the U.S. Supreme Court hadn't stopped the count. In making this claim, Moore chooses to ignore the most definitive post-election examinations of the ballots.

Two large news consortiums (*USA Today* and *The Miami Herald* headed one; the other included the *New York Times*) conducted massive recounts of Florida's ballots. Both reached very similar conclusions, and neither supported Moore's claim. To quote from the *USA Today* group's findings (May 11, 2001):

"Who would have won if Al Gore had gotten manual counts he requested in four counties? Answer: George W. Bush."
"Who would have won if the U.S. Supreme Court had not stopped the hand recount of undervotes, which are ballots that registered no machine-readable vote for president? Answer: Bush, under three of four standards."
"Who would have won if all disputed ballots—including those rejected by machines because they had more than one vote for president — had been recounted by hand? Answer: Bush, under the two most widely used standards; Gore, under the two least used."

Unless all these news organizations are part of Moore's vast right-wing conspiracy, his claim that the U.S. Supreme Court's reversal of the Florida Supreme Court's decision cost Gore the election is based only upon his own wishes, not facts.

Florida Governor Jeb Bush stole the election for his brother by removing African-American voters, who were likely to vote for Gore, from the rolls. Again, Moore ignores documented fact.

Some background: Florida bans felons from voting (unless they've been granted clemency). Before the 2000 vote, the state hired Database Technologies to purge rolls of felons and dead people. Some non-felons were erroneously removed from the rolls—but the errors didn't "target" minorities.

The liberal-leaning Palm Beach Post found that "a review of state records, internal e-mails of [Database Technologies] employees and testimony before the civil rights commission and an elections task force showed no evidence that minorities were specifically targeted."

The law against felon voting does have a racial impact, since African-Americans make up the greatest share of felons (nearly 49 % felons convicted in Florida). But the application of that law in 2000 skewed somewhat the opposite way — whites were actually the most likely to be erroneously excluded.

The error rate was 9.9% for whites, 8.7% for Hispanics, and only a 5.1% for African-Americans.

Michael Moore has been honest in one regard: He freely admits he hopes his film helps defeat President Bush this fall. It's hard to find much else that he's been honest about, however—including calling "Fahrenheit 9/11" a documentary.

Originally appeared July 12, 2004 in the New York Post.

Sampling of Entire State
Refutes Selective Error-Data

There is a corrosive perception that the voting system in parts of the United States systematically prevents people from voting and that this particularly discriminates against blacks. Litigation over punch-card voting machines tried unsuccessfully to derail the 2003 election in California to recall the governor, and now the American Civil Liberties Union (ACLU) has brought a similar lawsuit in Ohio.

The ACLU is not alone: As many as 18% of blacks nationally and 20% of 18- to 24-yearolds claim they don't believe their votes are counted accurately. Thus, this is a hard issue to ignore.

Since the 2000 Florida presidential election, the question has been how elections officials can prevent nonvoted, or so-called spoiled, ballots. These occur when voters either mark too many candidates (overvoting) in a race or do not vote for any candidate (undervoting).

Much of the debate centers on whether these nonvotes are intentional or the result of problems using punch-card machines.

Over the past three presidential elections in Ohio, punch cards have produced higher rates of nonvoted ballots than other voting machines do. Votomatic punch cards used in 69 of Ohio's 88 counties averaged a 2.4% nonvoted ballot rate. By comparison, electronic machines had a 1.1% rate, levers 1.5% and optical scans 2%.

The focus on the presidential race is understandable, given the experience in Florida, but it is also quite misleading. In races for Congress and state legislature, Votomatic machines actually do much better than electronic and lever machines and perform similarly to optical scans.

This result is natural, because voters simply don't know or care as much about other races as they do who wins the presidency. Interestingly, the drop-off in voting for other races is much less for punch cards than for other types of voting machines. For example, compared with the 1.3% difference between voting systems in presidential races, the nonvoted ballot rate for Ohio Senate races for Votomatic machines is almost 10%, while the rates for electronic and lever machines is 18%.

Even after accounting for factors that could affect nonvoted ballot rates, such as income and education and the number of candidates in a race, switching from Votomatic punch cards to electronic or lever machines would result in about 200 more nonvoted ballots in the average Ohio ward of 1,696 voters.

This pattern has held true for decades. Even an expert hired by the ACLU, professor Herb Asher at Ohio State University, also found that punch-card machines overall had much lower rates of nonvoted ballots than other machines during the 1978 election. Once this was clear, the ACLU did not call him to testify during the trial in July.

Why punch cards do so well down the ballot is simple. The more effort or time it takes to vote, the fewer races voters vote in. For example, recent research points to problems with the electronic machines regarding "the willingness of voters to navigate through multiple ballot screens before casting a vote (and) delays caused by the use of the review feature when coupled with extended ballots." Whatever their faults, punch cards are relatively quick and simple to use.

Most important for the ACLU's case, my research found that Votomatic machines were the only ones that consistently had lower nonvoted ballot rates for blacks than for whites. The Datavote punch-card machines that were used by only one county in 2000 and optical scans used by 11 counties were the worst for blacks, with electronic and lever machines varying, depending upon which race one examined.

Yet, even then, the race of voters only explains a small 0.4% to 3% of the variation in nonvoted ballot rates, itself an already small number.

With all the debate over voting machines, one would think that they must be too complicated for many people to figure out. But neither education nor income is related to nonvoted ballot rates. For education, the nonvoted ballot rate is high for those with less than a ninth-grade education, low for those with some high school, high for high school graduates, low for college graduates and generally higher again for those with post-graduate degrees. Instead of deep conspiracy theories, some voters were probably more conflicted over whom to vote for and decided not to support anyone in some races.

My data, as well as Asher's, examine the entire state, not just a few counties, as all the experts the ACLU used did. Nor has the ACLU ever explained exactly why it thinks that blacks have a more difficult time using punch cards.

The ACLU's lawsuit seems designed to maximize confusion, not just in Ohio but across the nation. If it wins, then any close election at least could be challenged in the press.

But whatever short-term political gains, the unfounded claims of selective disenfranchisement risk poisoning the political debate for years to come.

Originally appeared August 17, 2004 in the Columbus Dispatch.

Voting Machine Conspiracy Theories

Electronic voting machines were billed as the wave of the future just months ago. But now, by today, California's Secretary of State Kevin Shelley will have to decide whether to ban them. Even if he doesn't, the Legislature is threatening to do so. Supposedly, electronic machines – being installed across the country – will allow all sorts of fraud.

This month Democrats on the U.S. Commission on Civil Rights joined the chorus against electronic voting machines claiming: "We're ending up in '04 with the very same problems and issues that were there before."

Senators Hillary Clinton and Bob Graham, as well as Congressmen Rush Holt and Tom Davis recently introduced legislation to help prevent any fraud by requiring that electronic machines have paper-recording devices. Florida Congressman Robert Wexler has even brought a lawsuit because he worries that the Bush brothers will steal the election again, this time using electronic machines.

State and federal governments are spending billions of dollars to replace punch card machines with electronic machines. Yet, instead of improving the election process, the claims of fraud may poison the political debate for years to come.

Bill Maher's jokes may be funny: "Some 13-year-old hacker in Finland is going to hand the presidency to (singer) Kylie Minogue!" And, more seriously, Senator Clinton warns Democrats how "hacking" can easily "skew our elections" and points out that a Republican is the second largest manufacturer of electronic voting machines.

While scary, the stories have one major problem: none of the systems is hooked up to the Internet. The electronic voting machines are stand-alone units. It would be like someone trying to hack into your computer while it wasn't hooked up to the Internet. Impossible.

After the election, most electronic voting machines transfer the election results to a compact disk or some other "read only" format. These CDs are then taken to a central location where they are read into a computer. In the 20-plus years that these machines have been used, in many counties all across the country, there has never been a verified case of tampering.

When computer scientists warn of possible tampering with voting machines, they are not talking about hacking but about someone physically breaking open the lock on each individual machine and reprogramming it. Even if those breaking into the machines overcome the tamper-proof seals without being noticed, going through one computer at a time hardly seems like the way to steal most elections.

What about the nightmare scenario that a Republican manufacturer will secretly program the computers in advance to alter the election? Suppose that such a tampering scheme were to occur. Such tampering would easily be revealed as the precinct election workers check the machines for accuracy with sample votes both before and after the election.

Some machines are even randomly chosen to test during the day just in case their programs were set to only miscount votes during voting hours. If the programming switches, say, one out of every 10 votes, it would show up when sample votes are fed into the machines.

A few electronic voting machines, along with even more optical scans, offer election officials the option to collect vote counts using encrypted modems in addition to removable read-only memory. Michael Wertheimer, a security expert commissioned by the state of Maryland to evaluate electronic voting security, reportedly "broke into the computer at the state Board of Elections" during a test and "completely" changed the election results.

Yet, the tampering wasn't under real-world conditions, used an old system and really didn't change the results. Not only does a hacker have to know what telephone number to call, bypass the modem encryption and determine the password within a very narrow time frame, but two sets of calls reportedly from the same precinct would raise a red flag. Even if all those things go wrong, the original data in the voting machines would not be compromised, and it would still be possible to conduct an accurate recount.

Interestingly, no politicians so far have raised these same concerns about optical scans even though this threat involves hacking a central computer, not electronic voting machines.

Paper ballots add nothing, except generating unnecessary costs.

Possible computer crashes or corrupted data are taken care of by multiple redundant memory systems, some of which cannot be altered but are "read only." These memories are constantly checked for any differences.

The irony is that the politicians who complained the loudest about how punch card machines and hanging chads in Florida disenfranchised voters are now complaining the loudest about what they earlier insisted was the "cure." Conspiracy theories may rally the political faithful but at the risk of even greater hostility and mistrust among voters.

Originally appeared April 30, 2004 in the San Diego Tribune.

Let the Market Work Even During Disasters

Distraught over the loss of their homes from Hurricane Charley, some Floridians have turned their anger on "price gougers." $8,000 for removing a fallen tree from a yard? $5 bags of ice? $3 for gasoline? Newspapers carry stories of an 80-year-old woman who was told when she first called a hotel that a room cost $45, but by the time she called back it was going for $61. How can anyone justify such prices?

By last Wednesday, almost 1,900 price-gouging complaints had been filed with the state Attorney General's office for everything from hotel rooms to gas to lumber to ice. Governor Jeb Bush denounces these higher prices as "horrific." Republican state Attorney General Charlie Crist started bringing some suits within a day of complaints.

But to the extent that government successfully suppresses prices, it is Floridians who will suffer, not just now but after future hurricanes as well.

EMPTY SHELVES

Higher prices force people to economize, create incentives for companies to provide more and do it quickly, and make sure that people who value products the most get them. Do we really want to show up at the store and find nothing there?

• $8,000 for a fallen tree might seem extreme, but homeowners have an alternative: wait a couple of weeks. Right now fallen trees are all over the place. There are more trees than there are people to remove them. Some fallen trees are more dangerous than others and should be removed more quickly. If prices are not allowed to rise above what they were before the hurricane, people who should wait, and save a few dollars, won't.
• People will be more sparing with how they use a $5 bag of ice than if they cost $1. Without air conditioning and refrigeration, everyone during August in Florida wants ice. But at a dollar a bag, stores would find themselves quickly sold out. The first

people at a store will take bags even if it means just lowering their temperatures from already comfortably cool levels to cold.

• No one wants their grandmother to pay more for a hotel, but we all also want to have our grandmothers have some place to stay. As the price of hotel room's rise, some may decide that they will share a room with others. Instead of a family getting one room for the kids and another for the parents, some will make do with having everyone in the same room. At high enough prices, friends or neighbors who can stay with each other will do so.

You would think that people had learned their lessons about price controls during the 1970s. Price controls don't stop the cost of goods from rising. They just change how we pay for them. Chronic shortages of gasoline had Americans waiting in lines for hours. We seemingly tried everything. California adopted a rule that limited people's purchases to those days when the last digit of their license plate coincided with whether the calendar date was odd or even. Yet, the supposedly permanent shortages disappeared instantly as soon as Ronald Reagan removed price controls.

GREED IS GOOD

There is another side to this problem. Companies in states all across the south, hoping to make a few dollars, loaded up their trucks with food, water, and generators. The higher the prices, the faster these "greedy" companies and individuals got their products down to customers. But their greed meant less suffering. The more products delivered, the less prices rose.

Yet, it is not just current customers who suffer from these "temporary" price controls. Victims of future hurricanes face a rougher time as well.

Why do grocery stores decide how much food to keep in inventory? One reason is the oft chance that some future disaster dramatically and quickly increases demand. The more a disaster might create shortages and raises prices, the more it will pay for a grocery store to add in that additional refrigerator.

The refrigerator, space, and inventories cost money. If the storm doesn't hit, they will have extra food they won't sell. Take away the chance to cover these costs and companies won't make those investments.

What about the poor? Making the companies pay for others altruism not only creates the wrong incentives, it is also unfair. If we need to help out, make everyone pay. In any case, by Tuesday, the federal government was already handing out money so people could buy food and rent hotel rooms.

We'd all like lower prices, not just during disasters, but all the time. Yet, banning price increases doesn't solve the problem, it only hides it.

Bashing companies may be profitable short-term political behavior, but, unfortunately, these same politicians probably won't be around to accept the blame for the greater problems these regulations create down the road.

Originally appeared August 24, 2004 in Investors' Business Daily.

Statistical Mishmash
Muddles Unemployment Rates

It is puzzling. The unemployment rate keeps on falling, but there doesn't seem to be any new jobs. The press reports on "America's struggling job market," while from June to December last year the unemployment rate fell from 6.4% to 5.7%.

We are said to be in a "jobless recovery." Supposedly, the unemployment rate keeps falling because people have simply given up looking for jobs. However, the real answer is quite simple: numbers are being mixed and matched from different sources with little notion of how they are calculated.

The Department of Labor provides two different sets of labor market statistics: the *Establishment Survey* and the *Household Survey*. The *Establishment Survey* polls 400,000 companies on how many employees they have. The *Household Survey* questions 60,000 households each month on whether they have jobs and whether someone is looking for one.

There are a number of technical reasons that the two surveys can yield different numbers. For example, people with more than one job will be counted multiple times in the establishment survey. On the other hand, the self-employed are only counted by the household survey.

The so-called "jobless recovery" (search) picture is painted using the *Household Survey* for calculating the unemployment rate but using the *Establishment Survey* for the number of jobs created. The *Household Survey* can be used for both measures as it, too, provides estimates on the total number of people employed. But the two surveys have implied dramatically different changes in employment over the last few years. Over the last year, the *Household Survey* shows that almost two million new jobs have been created, while the *Establishment Survey* indicated a job loss of 62,000 jobs. Over the entire Bush administration, the *Household Survey* found that about 2.4 million new jobs have been created. By contrast, the *Establishment Survey* shows a net addition of only 522,000.

Why the difference? The number of companies does not

remain fixed. Old firms die and new ones are born. The *Establishment Survey* finds out about the company deaths quickly, but it takes longer to learn about births. The current list of firms surveyed excludes firms started over almost the entire last two years. What the *Establishment Survey* shows is that total employment in older firms has changed little over the last three years. It completely missed the growth in new jobs among new startups and self-employment.

Not surprisingly, the choice of numbers is central to the political debate. Using the *Establishment Survey*, Democratic presidential candidates charge that over two million jobs have been lost under the Bush administration from January 2001 to January 2003. Yet, as noted earlier, the inclusion of more recent numbers now indicate a small net addition. Eventually Democrats will be forced to update their claims.

The confusion over these numbers crosses party lines. Just on Sunday, conservative George Will asked: "Do we even have to think whether these jobs are coming back?" In interviews over the weekend, both Vice President Dick Cheney and Treasury Secretary John Snow failed to even mention, let alone explain, the different estimates.

Part of the problem may simply be the complicated nature of these numbers. The *Establishment Survey* is much larger, surveying 400,000 businesses, compared to the 60,000 households used by the other survey. The *Establishment Survey* makes the claim of being more comprehensive, but the Household Survey is still quite large and it has always been the "official" measure for calculating the unemployment rate. The systematic bias in the *Establishment Survey* is what is important: it completely ignores new startup businesses, and we have had an usually large expansion in this category over the last couple of years.

By only referring to the *Establishment Survey* numbers, the media has implicitly taken sides in the debate, albeit perhaps unknowingly. A simple Nexis computer search of the news media from Nov. 1, 2003, to Jan. 10 finds 975 stories using the term "jobless recovery" to describe the U.S. economy.

This last week, news stories carried such headlines as "Unemployment Rate Falls, But Analysts See Little Good News in Report" (*Dallas Morning News*) to "Democrats Zero In on 'Pathetic' Jobs Report" (*Los Angeles Times*) to "U.S. Economy Is Mired in a

Jobless Recovery" (*Miami Herald*). A fresh group of newspaper headlines quickly followed with headlines on "Where Do Jobs Go in Global Economy?" Even London's *Financial Times* ran such headlines as "America's 'Jobless Recovery' Leaves Economists Lost for Words" and "Employment Figures Throw U.S. Revival Into Doubt."

Given this rhetoric, it hard to believe that the current 5.7% unemployment rate is lower than the average unemployment rates during the 1970s (6.4%), 1980s (7.3%) or 1990s (5.8%).

All is not lost. Eventually the *Establishment Survey* numbers will be adjusted for all the new startups that have sprung up over the last couple of years. Unfortunately, much of this won't be reported until after the 2004 elections when all but a handful of historians and economists will pay attention.

Originally appeared January 14, 2004, at FoxNews.com.

Does Release Of Terror Info
Do More Harm Than Good?

What did we gain by telling the terrorists we know exactly which five targets in D.C., New York and New Jersey they were planning to blow up?

After all the late-night TV jokes trying to figure out what the different vague terrorist color alerts mean, many find comfort in having such specific information made public, but it is a false feeling of safety.

While those five targets are undoubtedly safer, we have likely lost an important informational advantage and left new targets more vulnerable than the original ones.

Can you imagine past wars if we had let the enemy know we had broken its codes before a major battle? How would World War II have turned out if we had let the Japanese know we knew of their carrier movements before Midway?

Some security experts, such as Vince Cannistraro, a former CIA counterterrorism chief, praised Homeland Security Secretary Tom Ridge's announcement: "If I worked in one of those buildings, I would feel very safe now. Given that it's captured material and now made public, there's a good chance it won't happen."

Well, by that logic, Midway also could have been prevented.

SWITCH TARGETS

Last week, President Bush reiterated his promise to keep releasing this information. Over the weekend Rep. Jane Harmon, the ranking Democrat on the House Intelligence Committee, and Democratic Sen. Charles Schumer demanded that such information continue to be released.

But two points are clear: terrorists can change their plans, and there are a lot of vulnerable targets. The five listed targets are financial centers: the New York Stock Exchange (NYSE), Citigroup bank, Prudential Financial and international aid agencies located in Washington.

The NYSE is an obvious target. But there are important financial centers, such as the Chicago Board of Trade, in other cities. Citigroup is the largest bank in the world and an attractive target. But even among U.S. banks, there are other attractive targets.

And what are terrorists to make of Ridge's statement that there is no information about attacks against financial targets in Chicago, San Francisco or Los Angeles?

FOCUS RESOURCES

If the terrorists behave like common criminals, one thing is certain: They move when enforcement gets hot. When police target drug dealing or prostitution in one part of town, these crimes don't stop. They move someplace else. Even when you let citizens carry concealed handguns, part of the local drop in crime is from criminals moving to nearby areas that do not let people protect themselves.

If Ridge's announcement leads to a change in where the attack takes place, we lose an important informal advantage. Would you rather have an attack on a specific target we know of in advance or have an attack on one we don't?

At least if you know terrorists are going to try to blow up a particular building, you can put all your resources around that building to stop them in the act.

With revelations that there were 10 other buildings that had been cased by the terrorists, it doesn't seem that replanning truck or car bombs will be that difficult.

Some might fear that by involving local police, our information will leak out. If so, we would then be in the same position we are now.

Getting the public to take the general threat seriously and putting people on alert is something everyone values, as long as we are putting them on alert in the right place. An attack that occurs at a different target than those announced only undermines getting people to be vigilant in the future.

Even if special untold circumstances justify the information being released, Bush and Ridge's promise that "when we have specific credible information we will share it" makes no sense as a general rule.

The capture of Muhammad Naeem Noor Khan, who Pakistani intelligence say operated a secret al-Qaida communications system, is a major breakthrough in the war on terrorism and gave the administration the information behind its warning. But clearly the terrorist cells that were to attack the financial targets are still out there.

The question is: What are the odds that we will again discover their plans before they strike their new target?

Politics played an important role in Ridge's announcement, though not the role that Democrats claim. The firestorm that would erupt if a president knew of an impending attack and didn't announce it would be devastating. The same trade-off exists for any public official.

Yet what is politically the right answer isn't always the right answer for stopping an attack.

CHOOSING THE LOWEST RISK

Those used as "bait" would be justifiably angry, but the question is what actions will save the most lives. Unfortunately, the political calculus seems clear: It is far better politically for a president to honestly say he put out the information he had, even he failed to stop an attack on what turned out to be the new target.

With Democratic surrogates such as Howard Dean on TV claiming that Ridge's announcement was simply designed to bolster Bush's political support and prominent Democrats embracing Michael Moore's conspiracy theories, a low political risk strategy may be the only possibility. But low-risk politics is not the same as low risk to lives.

Originally appeared August 17, 2004 in Investors' Business Daily.

Supreme Irrelevance:
Will the High Court Be Undone
by Political Reality?

When is a television station not a television station? How about if it is owned by the National Rifle Association? It may not seem momentous, but the NRA's announcement this week that it might buy a television or radio station has sent shockwaves through campaign-finance-regulation advocates and may ultimately undo last week's Supreme Court decision upholding McCain-Feingold. If the NRA were recognized as a media organization, it would be free to say what it wanted about political candidates, not constrained by any campaign-finance laws. No worries about restrictions on independent campaign expenditures.

General Electric or Time Warner or Viacom own television companies and can easily produce positive news coverage for favored candidates. No one would seriously think of limiting the number of their favorable news stories for a candidate or the ads that they could take out advertising the favorable show. But right now the NRA is not the media and without getting a media exemption, the campaign-finance laws restrict what radio or television ads the NRA can run.

So what distinguishes the NRA from these companies? Surely, not that they are nonprofit. Churches own radio and television stations and publish newspapers.

Possibly the NRA is simply different because it has a well-known political opinion. But doesn't the *New York Times* or the *Washington Post* also have a well-known stance on gun control? Newspapers can run an editorial or news stories supporting candidates any day. Unlike everyone else, the media can mention a candidate's name during the 60 days before the general election. Yet, the NRA is forbidden from placing an ad next to the editorials in those very same newspapers.

It is not even really clear whether the NRA even has to buy a television station to qualify as part of the media. The NRA already is one of the biggest magazine publishers in the country, with about a dozen publications, and provides news on their website.

Just this September when the Supreme Court heard the

challenges to the newest campaign-finance rules (the McCain-Feingold law), Justice Anthony Scalia anticipated this problem with campaign finance. During the oral arguments he noted: "if history teaches us anything, [it] is that when you plug one means of expression, the money will go to whatever means of expression are left."

By trying to become part of the media, the NRA has shown ultimate unenforceability of campaign-finance rules.

Not surprisingly, the NRA's actions have generated outrage. Senator John Kerry demanded that the Federal Election Commission block any attempt by the NRA to get a media exemption claiming: "We urge you to prevent the NRA from hijacking America's airwaves with the gun lobby's money."

It has been a brutal couple of months for campaign-finance reform. Democratic presidential candidates have abandoned public financing. Candidates who have long claimed the system necessary for helping challengers now say when their own campaigns are on the line that public financing entrenches incumbents.

Campaign-finance reform will undoubtedly also survive recent scandals. Even the revelation of a Brooklyn city-council candidate who was apparently the first to realize that you could use donations to get matching funds and then hire those same donors as political consultants with the government money. With New York City offering four dollars of matching funds for every dollar raised, few legal investments provide that kind of return.

Others have noted that if Governor Dean, Senator Kerry, and President Bush hadn't opted out of the public-finance system, the program would be out of money now. Taxpayers have simply been unwilling to even redirect some of the taxes that they have to pay anyway into the system. When you have the Federal Election Commission just announcing that Lyndon LaRouche, the perennial conspiracy-theorist candidate and convicted felon, will soon get a check from the government for $840,000, taxpayer distaste for the system is quite understandable.

Yet, despite these various problems, the events surrounding the NRA this week may be something quite different — the effective end of campaign-finance regulations. News organizations will rightly claim that they cannot do their jobs if campaign-finance regulations are applied to them. Surely even the liberal majority on the Supreme Court will realize that regulating the content of news stories or stopping the media from advertising their shows goes too far.

But what really distinguishes General Electric's versus General Motors's ability to influence elections? Is it really simply GE's ownership of television networks? Can Unions buy radio stations? Can anyone possibly rationalize such distinctions?

It looks like Scalia was right. Before the Supreme Court's decision was even issued last week to uphold McCain-Feingold parts of the regulations were already coming apart.

Originally appeared December 19, 2003 in National Review Online.

Baghdad's Murder Rate
Irresponsibly Distorted

Defense Secretary Donald Rumsfeld created quite a ruckus this June when he said: "You've got to remember that if Washington, D.C., were the size of Baghdad, we would be having something like 215 murders a month."

This bothered some simply because it indicated that Iraq was being handled well. But another aspect upset many: that a country where civilians were able to freely own machine guns could have a lower murder rate than our own nation's capital where even handguns are banned.

The claim did not sit well with those pushing to renew the assault weapons ban in our own country.

SOUNDS DANGEROUS

The apparently low crime rate was all the more surprising because Saddam Hussein had let all Iraq's criminals out of jail before his government was removed. In addition, Iraq is still in turmoil: Iraqi police are new to their jobs and terrorist attacks stretch them thin.

The debate over Baghdad's crime just resurfaced, with the *New York Times* publishing an op-ed by two Brookings Institution researchers, Adriana Lins de Albuquerque and Michael O'Hanlon. It claims that Baghdad's murder rate is among the highest in the world. Supposedly Baghdad's annualized murder rate from April to October this year ranged from an incredible 100 to 185 per 100,000 people—a number, they pointed out, that averaged several times greater than the rate in Washington.

Even an op-ed in the U.S. edition of the *Wall Street Journal* by retired General Barry McCaffrey says that Rumsfeld is in "denial" when he claims the "crime levels" are comparable in the two cities. An AP story points to bodies in the morgue and claims "Baghdad is in the midst of an unprecedented crime wave."

Yet, according to the *Wall Street Journal Europe*, the U.S. Army 1st Division in Baghdad reports that the numbers fell continually from a high of 19.5 per 100,000 in July to only 5 per 100,000 in October. The October rate is actually lower than the 5.6 U.S. murder rate in 2002.

By contrast, the *New York Times*' latest numbers for October claim to show a murder rate of 140—a difference of 28-fold.

Albuquerque and Michael O'Hanlon not only imply that murders are rampant, but generally rising. By contrast, the U.S. Army 1st Division's numbers show crime is under control and falling, vindicating Rumsfeld. The murder rate would then never be even half as high as that for Washington, D.C. If Albuquerque and Michael O'Hanlon are right, Rumsfeld has some serious explaining to do.

SO WHO IS RIGHT?

I contacted the authors of both pieces. Adriana Lins de Albuquerque and Michael O'Hanlon, who wrote the *Times* piece, provided two sources for their murder rate numbers: an article by Neil MacFarquhar in the September16 *New York Times* and a piece by Lara Marlowe in the October 11 *Irish Times*.

Both references clearly stated that much more than murder was included in the reports that they used from the Baghdad morgue.

MacFarquhar notes that these deaths also included "automobile accidents" and cases where people "were shot dead by American soldiers," cases that clearly did not involve murders.

The *Irish Times* piece mentions that "up to a quarter of fatal shootings [in the morgue] are caused by U.S. Troops."

For some perspective, in D.C., murders account for fewer than 5% of all deaths.

Even counting only the types of deaths explicitly mentioned in the stories citing the Baghdad morgue (accidental deaths, murders, suicides) and assuming that soldiers were engaged in the same type of fighting in D.C. as they are in Iraq, murders in D.C. would account for just a third of deaths.

The respective numbers for the U.S. as a whole are even lower: a half of one percent and 11%.

INFLATED SUMS

Obviously, counting these other deaths as "murders" in D.C. would imply that murders were three to 20 times more common than they actually were.

A public affairs officer with that division, Jason Beck, confirmed for me that a large part of the Iraqi legal system is being overseen by the U.S. JAG officers, and they are using the same standards for murder rates as used in the U.S. and separating out murders from other deaths.

Numbers mean a lot. Perceptions that conditions in Iraq are deteriorating constantly gets play in evaluating whether President Bush deserves re-election.

When a publication of record such as the *New York Times* gets Baghdad's October murder rates wrong by up to a factor of 28 to 1 and no correction is issued, the consequences are significant. To equate accidental deaths and U.S. soldiers killing terrorists with murders is irresponsible.

Originally appeared December 12, 2003, in Investors' Business Daily.

Let the Sunshine In:
the Same Old Myths Live on
About Florida, November 2000

Headlines this weekend recited the old line "Dems accuse Bush of stealing the 2000 election." Former U.S. Representative Carrie Meek received a wildly enthusiastic response from delegates to the Florida Democratic convention with calls that "We should be ready for revenge!" Retired General Wesley Clark told delegates he fought for democracy and free elections in Vietnam and Europe only to see "the taking" of the presidency by Republicans in 2000. Senator John Edwards said, "We had more votes; we won!" Senator John Kerry of Massachusetts said: "None of us are going to forget." More vaguely, Senator Joe Lieberman claimed that Bush "stretched the truth" to get his way in 2000. Of course, Terry McAuliffe was beating the same old drum. They should all get over it.

The stolen election supposedly incorporated many wrongs, but foremost was discrimination against Democratic African-American voters: Faulty voting machines were said to have thrown out their votes at higher rates. Also included are claims that the voters' intent wasn't properly divined, that Republicans on the Supreme Court felt compelled to covertly snatch the election, and that African-Americans were intimidated into not voting or were erroneously placed on the ineligible list at higher rates than other racial groups.

These charges have been rebutted before, but with so much misinformation and people's short memories simply accepting the charges, many risk believing that they are true. There has also been new research—which most people may not be aware of—which helps replace myth with reality.

THE MYTH OF THE FLAWED VOTING MACHINES
& DEMOCRATIC DISENFRANCHISEMENT

Suppose spoiled or non-voted ballots really did indicate disenfranchisement, rather than voter preferences. Then according to the precinct-level vote data compiled by *USA Today* and other newspapers, the group most victimized in the Florida voting was African-American Republicans, and by a dramatic margin, too.

I published an article in the Journal of Legal Studies analyzing the *USA Today* data, and it shows that African-American Republicans who voted were 54 to 66 times more likely than the average African American to cast a non-voted ballot (either by not marking that race or voting for too many candidates). To put it another way: For every two additional black Republicans in the average precinct, there was one additional non-voted ballot. By comparison, it took an additional 125 African Americans (of any party affiliation) in the average precinct to produce the same result.

Some readers may be surprised that black Republicans even exist in Florida, but, in fact, there are 22,270 such registered voters— or about one for every 20 registered black Democrats. This is a large number when you consider that the election in the state was decided by fewer than 1,000 votes. Since these Republicans were more than 50 times more likely to suffer non-voted ballots than other African Americans, the reasonable conclusion is that George W. Bush was penalized more by the losses of African-American votes than Al Gore.

Democrats have also claimed that low-income voters suffered non-voted ballots disproportionately. The data decisively reject this conclusion. For example, the poorest voters, those in households making less than $15,000 a year, had non-voted ballots at less than one-fifteenth the rate of voters in families making over $500,000.

It is difficult to believe that wealthy people were more confused by the ballot than poor people. Perhaps the rich or black Republicans simply did not like the choices for president and so did not vote on that part of the ballot. Perhaps there was tampering, but it is difficult to see how it could have been carried out and covered up. We may never know, but, clearly, the figures show that income and race were only one-third as important in explaining non-voted ballots as the methods and machines used in voting. For example, setting up the names in a straight line appears to produce many fewer problems than listing names on different pages or in separate columns.

THE MYTH THAT AFRICAN AMERICANS WERE INCORRECTLY PLACED ON THE CONVICTED-FELONS LIST AT A HIGHER RATE THAN OTHER GROUPS

The evidence on convicted felons comes from the U.S. Civil Rights Commission's *Majority Report*, which states: "The chance of being placed on this list [the exclusion list] in error is greater if the voter is African-American." The evidence they provide indicates that African-Americans had a greater share of successful appeals. However, since African-Americans also constituted an even greater share of the list to begin with, whites were actually the most likely to be erroneously on the list (a 9.9% error rate for Whites versus only a 5.1% error rate for blacks). The rate for Hispanics (8.7%) is also higher than for blacks. The Commission's own table thus proves the opposite of what they claim. A greater percentage of Whites and Hispanics who were placed on the disqualifying list were originally placed there in error.

In any case, this evidence has nothing to do with whether people were in the end improperly prevented from voting, and there are no data presented on that point. The *Majority Report*'s evidence only examines those who successfully appealed and says nothing about how many of those who didn't appeal could have successfully done so.

THE MYTH THAT GORE WOULD HAVE WON IF RECOUNT HAD BEEN ALLOWED

There were two news consortiums conducting massive recounts of Florida's ballots. One group was headed by *USA Today* and the *Miami Herald*. The other one was headed by eight news groups including the *Washington Post, New York Times, L.A. Times, Chicago Tribune*, the Associated Press, and CNN. Surprisingly, the two groups came to very similar conclusions. To quote from the USA Today group's findings (May 11, 2001) on different recounts:

Who would have won if Al Gore had gotten the manual counts he requested in four counties? Answer: George W. Bush.

Who would have won if the U.S. Supreme Court had not stopped the hand recount of undervotes, which are ballots that registered no machine-readable vote for president? Answer: Bush, under three of four standards.

Who would have won if all disputed ballots—including those rejected by machines because they had more than one vote for president—had been recounted by hand? Answer: Bush, under the two most widely used standards; Gore, under the two least used.

Of course, Florida law provided no mechanism to ask for a statewide recount a la the last option, only county-by-county recounts. And of course neither Gore's campaign nor the Florida Supreme Court ever asked for such a recount.

DON'T FORGET THE EARLY MEDIA CALL

Florida polls were open until 8 P.M. on election night. The problem was that Florida's ten heavily Republican western-panhandle counties are on Central, not Eastern, time. When polls closed at 8 P.M. EST in most of the state, the western-panhandle polling places were still open for another hour. Yet, at 8 Eastern, all the networks (ABC, CBS, CNN, FOX, MSNBC, and NBC) incorrectly announced many times over the next hour that the polls were closed in the entire state. CBS national news made 18 direct statements that the polls had closed.

Polling conducted after the election indicates that the media had an impact on voter behavior, and that the perception of Democratic wins discouraged Republican voters. Democratic strategist Bob Beckel concluded Mr. Bush suffered a net loss of up to 8,000 votes in the panhandle after Florida was called early for Gore. Another survey of western-panhandle voters conducted by John McLaughlin & Associates, a Republican polling company, immediately after the election estimated that the early call cost Bush approximately 10,000 votes.

Using voting data for presidential elections from 1976 to 2000, my own empirical estimates that attempted to control for a variety of factors affecting turnout imply that Bush received as many as 7,500 to 10,000 fewer votes than he would normally have expected. Little change appears to have occurred in the rate that non-Republicans voted.

Terry McAuliffe clearly stated his strategy "to use the anger and resentment that will come out of that 2000 election, put it in a positive way to energize the Democratic base." Democrats have used the notion that Bush is an illegitimate president to justify everything from their harsh campaign rhetoric to their filibusters against his judicial appointments.

More could be said about these myths, but most of them hardly merit discussion. Unfortunately, as Terry McAuliffe implies, these falsehoods will continue to be trumpeted frequently over the next year; thankfully, a few facts can help dispel them.

Originally appeared December 10, 2003 in National Review Online.

Rush, by the Numbers:
The Face of "Social Concern"?

Is it possible to even discuss race in sports, let alone anywhere else? This past week provides little hope. Whether Rush Limbaugh's comments on Donovan McNabb were "racist," there is a general agreement that he was factually wrong, that Limbaugh did not know what he is talking about. But what is the evidence?

Limbaugh readily admits that it was just his opinion that "the media has been very desirous that a black quarterback do well." But his critics allowed no possibility for uncertainty, calling his comments "ignorant" or worse. As National Public Radio put it: "Rush was able to turn a complete lack of understanding of football into a cross burning." Even the *Wall Street Journal* ran an editorial disagreeing with his statements on news coverage.

A couple of stories compared McNabb to another quarterback, such as Tampa Bay's Brad Johnson, whom many apparently regard as just a so-so quarterback. But no one has tried to compare the news coverage of any two quarterbacks, let alone generally between black and white quarterbacks in the NFL.

To measure positive news coverage, I quickly put ten research assistants to work on a Nexis search, a computerized search of newspaper stories across the country. They looked at the coverage received by the 36 quarterbacks who played during the first four weeks of this season. (The articles were from the day of their first game to the day after their last game during the period.) To try to make the categorization of news stories objective, 23 phrases were picked to identify positive descriptions of a quarterback and 23 phrases for negative ones. Positive phrases included words such as "brilliant," "agile," "good," "great," "tough," "accurate," "leader," "intelligent," or "strong arm." Negative phrases included "overrated," "erratic," "struggling," "bad," "weak arm," or "mistakes." Obviously the media involves more than newspapers, but this is measurable and it is not clear why newspapers would be so different from the rest of the media.

We then identified news stories where these phrases appeared within 50 words of a quarterback's name. Each story was read to check that the phrases were indeed used to describe the "quarterback" and to make sure that the word "not" did not appear before the different phrases. Depending on whether positive or negative words were used to describe the quarterback, stories were classified as positive, negative, or falling into both categories.

The evidence suggests that Rush is right, though the simplest measures indicate that the difference is not huge. Looking at just the averages, without trying to account for anything else, reveals a ten% difference in coverage (with 67% of stories on blacks being positive, 61% for whites).

We also collected data by week for each of the first four weeks of the season on a host of other factors that help explain the rate at which a player is praised: the quarterback's rating for each game; whether his team won; the points scored for and against the team; ESPN's weekly rank for the quarterback's team and the opponent; and whether it was a Monday night game. In addition, I accounted for average differences in media coverage both in the quarterback's city and the opponent's city as well as differences across weeks of the season.

Accounting for these other factors shows a much stronger pattern. Black quarterbacks' news coverage is 27% more positive than whites'. And that difference was quite statistically significant—the chance of this result simply being random is the same odds as flipping a coin five times and getting heads each time.

The quarterback ranking, scoring, winning, and higher-ranked teams playing against each other all increase the percentage of positive stories. For example, each additional point scored by the quarterback's team raises the share of positive news coverage by about one percentage point. Being in the only game played on a particular day lowers the how positive the coverage was by about 12%, as more newspapers outside the home area cover the game the next day.

The media's interest in the number of black quarterbacks can also be seen in other, more explicit ways. Last season, out of 217 news stories discussing the race of professional quarterbacks, 194 mentioned whether an individual quarterback was black, only 23 if they were white. By contrast, for running backs and receivers—where the ratio of blacks to whites is even more lopsided, with blacks dominating—discussions of a player's race are virtually nonexistent. Only 6 stories mentioned that running backs were black and 10 that they were receivers, and the numbers discussing that they were white were 4 and 7 respectively.

These numbers also help address another possibility: whether newspapers write such supportive articles on black quarterbacks to encourage more racial diversity on the field. A preference for diversity doesn't seem to explain the data. In positions where whites are underrepresented they do not receive even a fraction of the extra attention that blacks do as quarterbacks. If indeed skin color results in significantly more positive coverage, doesn't that imply that the media, not Rush, might be racist? Presumably the media feels that coverage is justified, though it could mean that the press has too low expectations of blacks.

Hopefully the furor over Rush's statement will help us understand the media a little better. The evidence indicates that there is a lot to explain. The current fact-free name-calling hardly shows that sports have come to grip with race.

(I would like to thank Brian Blasé and Jill Mitchell for unusually dedicated research work on this piece.)

Originally appeared October 10, 2003 in Washington Times.

Divorcing Voters, Again:
Supreme Court Campaign-Finance Reform
Case Gets Heard

To supporters, the McCain-Feingold campaign finance reform merely fills in the loopholes in previous campaign finance laws. Like other government attempts at central planning, the law is incredibly complicated and results in unintended consequences. A special three-judge district court felt it necessary to issue an unheard of 1,600 page opinion. To try to sort things out, the Supreme Court will today consider four hours of oral arguments, longer than any other hearing since the last major campaign-finance law was argued there in November 1975.

The new law seems to cover just about everything. It restricts how much parties can give to candidates and what can be given to political parties. Contributions by minors are banned. Limits on individual contributions are being raised, but they are now adjusted by a formula that penalizes wealthy candidates from spending their own money. The law limits or bans advertising by outside groups, when the group mentions the name of candidates for federal office within 60 days of a general election or within 30 days of a primary. Even when politicians can appear at fundraisers is regulated.

Supporters predict that all these rules will reduce money's role in politics and make elections more competitive, reduce corruption, and encourage more people to vote. Of course, this is what was predicted for past campaign finance regulations. But instead of getting better, things have gotten worse.

ENTRENCHING INCUMBENTS

Donation limits entrench incumbents, who can rely on voters' greater familiarity with them, as well as use government resources, to help them campaign and generate news coverage. It is very difficult for challengers to raise a large number of small donations. Incumbents are at an advantage here, as they have had years to put together long mailing lists and make contacts. Allowing large donations would make it easier for newcomers to raise large sums from only a few sources.

The long start required for fundraising means that if a candidate falters, it is virtually impossible for other candidates to enter in at the last moment.

Election data since World War II shows the impact of these rules. Prior to 1976, when donation limits began, House members lost 12% of their races; after 1976, it was just 6%. And Senators moved from a 24% loss rate to 19%.

Research of state donation limits on all state senate primary and general election races, with data covering 1984 through the 2002 primaries, revealed the impact of state regulations that are similar to those in McCain-Feingold. The regulations raised incumbents' winning vote margin by at least 4 percent and the number of state senate candidates running for office fell by an average of about 20%.

Rules that limit the help that parties can offer new candidates provide the greatest incumbent protection. Unknown challengers are usually highly dependent on party support.

For the U.S. House and Senate between 1984 and 2000, challengers in the House received a four times greater share of their money than incumbents from their parties. In the Senate, challengers were about twice as dependent. Republican challengers were also more dependent on this help than Democrats. And the research on state senate races shows that restrictions on party donations produce the biggest increases in incumbent win margins.

"LOOPHOLES"

The 1974 reforms did nothing to stop the growth in campaign spending. McCain-Feingold will be no more successful. Regulations may change how the money is spent, such as moving it from the candidates to independent groups, but the total amount spent depends upon what is at stake. As government grows, the importance of winning office increases and so does spending.

When given a chance, donors would much prefer to give their donations to the candidate directly than to an independent organization simply because it provides a more consistent message to voters. Uncoordinated independent expenditures educate voters less per dollar spent.

With regulations, the possible loopholes are endless. Suppose independent groups were completely banned. Would that stop money from being spent on elections? Obviously not. Instead of political contributions, wealthy individuals or organizations can buy radio and television stations or newspapers. Unless the first amendment is completely gutted, there is no way to regulate the number of favorable news stories given to different candidates.

Hillary Clinton has also shown the way this year through another loophole. Should Simon and Schuster's million dollar promotional budget for her book be counted as a campaign donation? Undoubtedly, the money made Clinton appear to be a more attractive presidential candidate. John McCain likewise benefited from a book tour for *Faith of My Fathers*, his book that came out the fall before the 2000 primaries. Yet, no one thus far has proposed that politicians cannot write and promote books.

CORRUPTION

Under Buckley v. Valeo, the Supreme Court held that the only permissible constitutional basis for government regulation was concern over the appearance or incidence of corruption. Yet, the government's defense of McCain-Feingold basically relies on hard-to-interpret anecdotal evidence.

In passing the McCain-Feingold campaign finance regulations, public interest groups and the press insist that donors supposedly only give money to politicians to bribe them. There is little doubt that campaign contributions and voting records often go together. But few mention that donors may be giving to candidates for another reason: they share the candidate's views.

Fortunately, we can separate out these two motives. Consider a retiring politician. He has little reason to honor any "bribes," for re-election is no longer an issue. Even if earlier there were corrupting influences from donations, the politician would now have freedom to vote according to his own preferences. Therefore, if contributions indeed bribe politicians to vote against their beliefs, there ought to be a change in the voting record when the politicians decide to retire.

This proves not to be the case. Together with Steve Bronars of the University of Texas, I have examined the voting records of the 731 congressmen who held office for at least two terms during the 1975 to 1990 period. We found that retiring congressmen continued voting the same way as they did previously, even after accounting for what they do after their retirement or focusing on their voting after they announce their retirement.

Despite retiring politicians only receiving 15% of their preceding term's political action committee (PAC) contributions, their voting pattern remains virtually the same; on average, they only alter their votes during their last term on only one out of every 450 votes. And even then it is the opposite of what the "bribing" theory would predict.

The voting records also reveal that over their entire careers politicians are extremely consistent in how they vote. Those who are the most conservative or liberal during their first terms are still ranked that way when they retire. Thus the young politician who does not yet receive money from a PAC does not suddenly change when that organization starts supporting him.

The data thus indicate that politicians vote according to their beliefs, and supporters are giving money to candidates who share their beliefs on important issues.

A reputation for sticking to certain values is important to politicians. This is why political ads often attack policy "flip-flops" by the opponent—if a politician merely tells people what they want to hear, voters lack assurance that he will vote for and push that policy when he no longer seeks re-election. Voters rather trust politicians who show a genuine passion for the issues.

If donations were really necessary to keep politicians in line, why would individual donors ever give money to a politician who is running for office for the last time?

Some point to PACs or corporations giving money to competing candidates in the same races as evidence of influence buying, but this claim is based upon a mistaken understanding of the data. The vast majority of PACs are banned by their charters from giving money to both sides in a race. The few exceptions occur when their own members are in a race and they feel obligated to encourage their members to run for office. The confusion over the numbers often comes about because donations during primaries are often lumped together with donations made during a general election. Yet, while a PAC wants to try to get the best Republican and Democrat selected in their primaries, they will only support one of them in the general election.

Similar confusion exists over corporate donations. Corporations don't give money to candidates. What happens is that the people who work for corporations give the money and it is not surprising that some people who work for a company like Republicans and others like Democrats. It makes no sense to say that the "company" is supporting both sides.

CONCLUSION

Despite all the rhetoric, past federal and state regulations have only succeeded in protecting incumbents from competition and divorced voters further from the political process. We shouldn't expect a different outcome this time.

Originally appeared September 8, 2003 in The National Review Online.

The Drug World's Easy Riders

with James K. Glassman

For years, Americans have enviously eyed low drug prices just over the border in Canada, where strict price controls prevail as part of a socialized national healthcare system. Canadian drugs are cheaper by about two-fifths.

Now, Americans are getting fed up, and the U.S. Congress is moving to lift restrictions on importing drugs from Canada—or re-importing, since nearly all drugs are made in the U.S. in the first place. A key vote on this issue is scheduled for today in the House of Representatives.

The reason Canadians, and Europeans who have similar national-healthcare systems, are able to enforce price controls and benefit from the lower prices that result is that they are classic free riders. U.S.-based drug companies spend vast sums to develop new drugs, and Americans pay market prices for them. Once developed, drugs are reasonably inexpensive to produce and reproduce, and companies are willing to sell the medicines at a price that merely covers the marginal cost of manufacturing and distribution.

The Americans pay the fixed cost of R&D, and that is all important. Over the long haul, companies will not keep developing new drugs unless they can recoup the massive costs of research and regulatory approval. Incredibly, Americans, who comprise just 5% of the world's population, account for 50% of the world's spending on drugs. In effect, the U.S. is underwriting the cost of a critical chunk of the world's health care. If U.S. spending on drugs dropped sharply as a result of re-importation, drug companies would simply stop making new drugs.

Re-importation, which at first glance seems like a decent idea, would be a disaster for all concerned. Canadians and Europeans, who currently benefit from both low prices and continued research, would be killing the goose that's laying the golden eggs. But American consumers, too, would be hurt. While they would get the short-term windfall of lower prices, they would end up suffering and not living as long as they could have—since promising new therapies would never be developed.

The current system, as unfair as it appears, actually works relatively well. It would work better, of course, if the world paid market prices for drugs. But the system will collapse if re-importation becomes legal.

U.S. legislators who advocate such a change—many of them Republican—are acting irresponsibly. Still, their response to the clamor of constituents is understandable. In the end, the most effective opposition to re-importation may have to come from Canada and Europe, which have little gain and everything, including lives, to lose.

At the heart of the issue lies the cost of developing a new drug and overcoming the regulatory hurdles to bring it to market: $802 million on average, according to a study by Tufts University. Even then, only three in 10 market drugs produce enough revenues to match or exceed the average costs of research and development. R&D now totals $30 billion a year. Despite such high risks, drug companies in the past 25 years have developed powerful new therapies for conditions—including high cholesterol, sepsis, depression, Alzheimer's, HIV/AIDS and asthma—that had been difficult or impossible to treat in the past.

But imagine if the legislation passes and the Food and Drug Administration gives its assent to the safety of re-imported drugs. It will then be profitable for middlemen to buy drugs outside the U.S. and keep shipping them back until U.S. prices are driven down to the level of Canadian and European prices—which are low not just because of price controls but also because of government restrictions on their use and because Canadians and Europeans have lower incomes than Americans (Canada's per-capita GDP in 2001 was $22,000, and the EU's $20,900, compared with $35,000 for the U.S.).

In response, drug companies might stop selling drugs to countries that allow re-exportation. The companies may be able to control sales from Canada since it is such a small market—sales of Vioxx, the popular arthritis pain treatment, total $145 million in Canada vs. $2 billion in the U.S. But if re-importation comes from the large European market, firms would face revenue losses that could be tolerated only by drastically reducing R&D.

In effect, re-importation of drugs would import something else to the U.S.: price controls, where the lack of such practices is the oxygen that allows pharmaceutical research to thrive.

Drug-price controls are pernicious. While controls on oil and other products tend to be short-lived, as voters eventually object to the resulting shortages, the effects of drug regulations are more difficult to observe since they mainly affect medicines that haven't been invented yet.

Even if people realized that controls were preventing new drugs from being developed, the lags would make the controls difficult to remove. Customers would have to pay higher prices for years before they saw any benefits. Firms would have to be convinced that new controls would not be imposed as soon as the new drugs are released.

This lost innovation would have real health costs. A recent study by Frank Lichtenberg of Columbia University found that life expectancy in 52 countries increased by an average of almost two years between 1986 and 2000 and that launches of "new chemical entities" accounted for 40% of that gain.

If Canada and Europe paid market prices for drugs, even more pharmaceuticals would be available to fight disease and save lives around the world. But that's a fantasy; they won't. The best the world can hope for is a continuation of the current process, which is another example of how Americans, often maligned by others for their selfishness, are, in fact, carrying heavy burdens for the rest of the world.

U.S. consumers, however, are unhappy with the status quo. They ask plaintively why they have to pay $270 for the same dosage of Lipitor that's sold in Canada for $180. But if Americans paid less, the system that has helped the entire world live longer and healthier would come crashing down. The irony is that Canada and Europe—by opposing the folly of re-importation—may be the last effective line of defense in maintaining the system, however rickety and anomalous, that so dramatically improves the health of nations.

Originally appeared July 23, 2003 , in The Wall Street Journal Europe.

When Welfare is Disguised as a Tax Cut

The debate over taxes has gone off track. As often happens in Washington, it sounds like politicians are often not talking the same language. Confusion abounds over what constitutes a tax cut or a welfare payment.

Confusion exists over even simple facts such as whether the poor who would benefit from a proposed child tax credit actually pay any taxes. Republicans are even battling Republicans.

Let's take the simplest factual question first. House Republicans claim that poor individuals do not pay income taxes, so how can they get a "tax cut"?

Democrats respond that while the poor don't pay income taxes, they still pay social security and medicare taxes and should get a credit to compensate them for having to pay those taxes. The White House has taken sides dismissing House Republican objections, saying that "These families deserve help and [the President] wants to give it to them."

To most people, it probably appears that both sides are right, it just depends upon where you want to draw the line.

Yet, both sides are not right. The poor's payroll taxes are already more than subsidized by the income tax. The Earned Income Tax Credit was originally justified politically for precisely this reason.

GENEROUS REFUNDS

Take a family of four, where both the husband and wife work, where one child has just started college and the other is under age 18. Indeed even without any new credits, this family will get more back from the government than they pay for income, social security and medicare until they make over $30,000.

At $21,000, they still get over $2,200 back from the government, over and above what they were paying in social security and payroll taxes. Passing the proposed child "tax credit" for this family will increase this giveback by another $400 because they have one child under 18. The new credits will be available for people earning between $10,500 and $26,625.

In the 1990s, we finally reformed welfare and tried to rein in its costs, but today the Earned Income Tax Credit has so ballooned that it represents twice as much money as spent by the traditional federal welfare program, the Aid for Families with Dependent Children. While government welfare programs officially put time limits on how long people can get welfare, the federal tax system makes the welfare payments tax relief and makes them permanent. What we learned from the success of the time limit getting people off of welfare appears to have been forgotten.

WELFARE AS STIMULUS

President Bush's justifications for the his tax cuts have helped muddle the whole debate on taxes by claiming that simply giving people more money will stimulate the economy. Lost is the notion of creating incentives to get people to work (lowering marginal tax rates). Using the essentially Keynesian reasoning advanced for the tax cuts, now even welfare payments appear to qualify as a stimulus for economic growth.

Editorials in the *New York Times* talk of "fat cats" getting their tax cuts and that "there won't even be crumbs left over for the working folks." Somehow, a tax bill that ensures that high-income people will pay yet a greater share of the tax bill has been painted as unfair to poor people.

For that matter, the 2001 tax cut also shifted a greater share of the tax burden to higher income people. Even without the newest tax change, about 10 million more low-income people have been completely removed from having to pay income taxes from 2000 to 2003.

How many times can you pass transfer payments to offset payroll taxes? Apparently, the answer is more than once. Completely lost in these debates is the focus that Ronald Reagan brought to the issue of marginal rates. Without even the fig leaf of justifying the child tax credit as a tax cut for those paying payroll taxes, why not call the lump sum payment to low income people what it is: permanent welfare payments.

Originally appeared July 2, 2003, in Investor's Business Daily

Much Ado About Nothing

Calling for President Bush to apologize, Senator Tom Daschle angrily attacked Bush on the Senate floor last Wednesday for politicizing the war. Daschle said: "This is outrageous! Outrageous!"

Claiming that Bush questioned Democrats patriotism, Daschle referred to Hawaii's Senator Inouye, who lost an arm in World War II. That same day Senator Robert Byrd called President Bush's conduct "despicable."

Pretty heated rhetoric. Yet, this entire ruckus was based on something that never occurred. Only through the filter of the press—with incomplete, out-of-context quotes—was it possible for Democrats' claims about Bush to be taken seriously.

Daschle's evidence that Bush was questioning Democrats' patriotism and politicizing the war came from a *Washington Post* quote of a speech that Bush had just made in New Jersey. The Post reported: "Bush has suggested that Democrats do not care about national security, saying on Monday that the Democratic-controlled Senate is 'not interested in the security of the American people.'"

But was Bush criticizing Democrats? Consider a more complete quote of the president's speech:

> "The Senate is more interested in special interests in Washington and not interested in the security of the American people. I will not accept a Department of Homeland Security that does not allow this president and future presidents to better keep the American people secure. People are working hard to get it right in Washington, both Republicans and Democrats. See, this isn't a partisan issue."

The president criticized "the Senate"—specifically not Democrats—over the Homeland Security Bill. Bush never even mentioned that Democrats control the Senate. The criticism was really one of union-job regulations and union influence, something with which Democratic senators such as Zell Miller agree. Some of the press coverage corrected the misimpression that Bush was referring to the war with Iraq.

Accepting Senator Daschle's claim that he knew nothing about Bush's speech beyond the *Washington Post* article, he should have checked the quote before lashing out against the president on the Senate floor. But that was not the only problem. The original *Washington Post* article error was compounded many times over. On the broader issue of attacking Democrats virtually no one in the media got the story correct.

In the news coverage from Wednesday afternoon through Friday afternoon, a Nexis computer search of national television news broadcasts and major newspapers reveals that 178 separate stories carried the quote that raised Daschle's hackles. Whether it was ABC, NBC, CBS, CNN, *New York Times, USA Today, Washington Post, Chicago Tribune*, or a myriad of other news outlets (even some foreign publications) only the partial quote was reported. Yet, just three of these news stories mentioned the subsequent sentences (*Brit Hume's Special Report* on Fox News, the *Milwaukee Journal Sentinel*, and the *Pittsburgh Post-Gazette*). The Associated Press sent out a file with this additional text from Bush's speech, but with little effect.

It might be one thing to chalk up this blunder to sloppiness (possibly just reprinting Democrat press releases and not reading the speech themselves) or the Bush administration failing to inform the press what really happened. But neither explanation really applies here. One piece in the *Los Angeles Times* at least acknowledged that the Bush administration argued that the quote was taken "out of context," but it provided no details about what context was missing and left readers believing it was merely a Republican debating point.

At least some of the press did read Bush's speech even if they selectively relayed it to readers. Take the *New York Times*, the so-called newspaper of record. The Times reprinted Daschle's entire Senate floor remarks and excerpted some of Bush's speech, but somehow managed to cut off reprinting Bush's speech right before Bush praised hardworking "Republicans and Democrats."

The impact of these selective quotes is obvious. Ideally, Daschle's or Byrd's angry floor speeches would never have taken place. But if just the next few sentences in Bush's speech had been mentioned, no one would have taken them seriously. Amazingly the distortion was so effective that by the end of the week even some Republicans were breaking ranks with the president.

President Bush has tried hard to change the culture of Washington, to take out the political attacks and downplay the rhetoric. Clearly he can't win for trying. A speech where he praises "Republicans and Democrats" is selectively quoted and turned by into a political attack.

Laziness by the press can't explain why this debate took place. Possibly the press merely wants to create controversy or maybe some deeper bias is at work. In neither case is public discourse well served.

Originally appeared September 30, 2002, in The National Review Online.

Unequal Punishment

There won't be much suspense when Martha Stewart is sentenced this Friday. Judge Miriam Cedarbaum has little discretion in sentencing Ms. Stewart. The U.S. Sentencing Guidelines set the rules, and Ms. Stewart probably faces between 10 and 16 months in jail for her convictions on four counts. Such narrow ranges were set up to promote "fairness," and treat criminals who committed the same crime equally.

Even to those for whom the guilty verdict is reasonable, Ms. Stewart's case illustrates a criminal justice system badly out of whack. Ms. Stewart faces penalties that are so out of proportion to the crimes she committed, that one cannot help conclude that the system penalizes the well-to-do much more than poorer criminals who commit the same offenses.

Before the 1987 guideline, judges could sentence two criminals who'd committed the same crime to vastly different sentences: Ms. Stewart could have been let off with simple probation or given more than 10 years. But judges were rarely that arbitrary. In fact, denying judges discretion has made penalties less—not more—equal.

The reason is simple: the justice system imposes many types of penalties on criminals, but the sentencing guidelines only make sure that the prison sentences are equal. Beyond prison, criminals face financial penalties that largely depend on the criminal's wealth. In addition to fines and restitution, white-collar criminals face the loss of business or professional licenses and the ability to serve as an executive or director for a publicly traded company.

Ms. Stewart, for instance, will never again serve as president of Martha Stewart Living and she'll give up her $1.5 million annual salary. Her criminal fines could reach $250,000 while the restitution and penalties from civil actions (both from the Securities and Exchange Commission and shareholder suits) will be enormous. But that is still only a small part of the impact of her conviction, given her overwhelming importance to her company.

On the day Ms. Stewart was convicted, the stock soared from $13.70 to $17 as reports speculated that some type of deal had been struck limiting her prison sentence, only to see the stock plunge to $10.50 by the end of the day after she had been convicted. Her conviction changed the company's value by over $320 million just between that day's high and low. As Ms. Stewart owns 63% of the company, she personally suffered a loss of $203 million on that day. The other shareholders bore the rest of this loss, but soon after the criminal case is concluded, they will file civil suits against Ms. Stewart, forcing her to cover their losses.

Compare the penalties Ms. Stewart faces to those of, say, a drug dealer convicted of the same crimes of giving false information to investigators. Both would face the same prison sentence. But without any discernible assets, the dealer would escape the other financial penalties Ms. Stewart faces. If the dealer had a public defender, he'd even avoid paying a lawyer.

How can these two vastly different penalties for lying to federal investigators be considered comparable? Surely defendants such as Ms. Stewart can hope to offset these much higher penalties with highly skilled lawyers, but this by no means levels the field. Ms. Stewart's total financial penalty could easily amount to over $300 million dollars, while the drug dealer faces a negligible additional penalty on top of imprisonment.

Prior to the sentencing guidelines, judges frequently took into account these different penalties and made adjustments to somewhat equalize the total penalty. But no longer.

It is hardly ever fashionable to defend the wealthy—let alone wealthy criminals. Yet the gap in punishment is so enormous it is impossible to ignore. If fairness means that two people who commit the same crime should expect the same penalty, the current system is not merely unfair, it is unconscionable.

Originally appeared July 13, 2004 in the Wall Street Journal.

States May Regret Reforms

Prison deters crime. It also keeps violent criminals off the street. Research by economists consistently indicates that while most of the drop in violent crime during the 1990s occurred because of more arrests and convictions, longer prison sentences also played a role, albeit a lesser one.

As crime has fallen, we have had more and more resources devoted to catching and punishing fewer and fewer criminals. That further raises the likelihood of detection, punishment and reducing crime.

Unfortunately, after years of large increases in state government expenditures, many states face big deficits. Although expenditures on incarceration make up less than 4% of state budgets, the pressure to cut is still there. Some states are considering eliminating mandatory minimum sentencing, revisiting three-strike rules or reforming sentencing guidelines.

Whatever the budget implications, some welcome the changes simply because they believe many penalties are too harsh. A number of studies indicate that three-strike rules significantly reduce crime, and states that have implemented them experience thousands of fewer violent crimes. Stiffer penalties for repeat criminals may also be justified simply because there is less doubt that the party being punished is really guilty.

But not all increases in penalties are equally successful in reducing crime. Some misguidedly focus on how the crime is committed—such as with a gun—rather than on the crime itself. Criminals frequently enough can change the weapon used in a crime. Unfortunately, none of the studies examining statutory minimums for using a gun in a crime has found a significant reduction in violent rates.

Sentencing reforms have produced some perverse results. For example, the primary goal of sentencing guidelines was to reduce the disparity among criminals who committed the same crime. By equalizing only prison sentences, the guidelines make it impossible for judges to equalize the "total" penalty, which can include fines and restitution. How these are imposed can vary dramatically among criminals.

Sentencing can be improved, and some penalties are too high, but if the reformers get their way, expect one thing: higher violent crime rates.

Originally appeared July 1, 2003 in USA Today.

Don't Mess With Texas

Just three years ago, Texas Democratic legislators made national news when they fled to New Mexico and Oklahoma to avoid a quorum in the state's House of Representatives. Today, the Supreme Court reviews the partisan congressional redistricting that they failed to stop. Despite all the angry words spoken, the Republicans' gerrymandering has proven to be much less partisan than the Democratic gerrymandering it replaced. It is also less biased than gerrymandering in other states, making it hard for the Supreme Court to strike down the new district lines as unconstitutional.

Everyone acknowledges that congressional lines are drawn to benefit the party drawing the lines, but when does it go too far? In Vieth v. Jubelirer (2004), the Supreme Court appeared to say that state legislatures can be too partisan in redistricting, though not in the case before them, involving Pennsylvania. The court was not able to agree on how to even determine when improper gerrymandering occurs.

The current case (League of United Latin American Citizens v. Perry) isn't going to make this problem any easier: invalidating the Texas redistricting as too partisan would cause a flood of other legal challenges. In 2004, the first and only election that was held after the new boundaries went into effect, Democrats received 40% of the major party vote but only 34% of the seats. However, this gap is actually small—not only when compared to the numbers in Texas at least since 1980, but also when compared to other states. Even Pennsylvania's constitutionally acceptable gap was almost twice as large.

During the two decades when Democrats completely ran redistricting—from 1981 through the 2000—they averaged about 12% more seats than their portion of the popular congressional vote in Texas. Even when the courts redrew the district lines in 2002, the gap was eight%. Who can argue with a straight face that the 2004 results represent excessive Republican gerrymandering when the Democrats now only received six% fewer seats than their vote share?

In 1994, Democrats lost congressional seats nationwide during the Republican takeover of Congress and their vote share in Texas tumbled to just 43%, but they still managed to hold on to 63% of the

Texas congressional delegation. When states have only one or even a few seats, large gaps between vote share and the share of seats won are difficult to avoid. For example, with only two seats, if one party gets two-thirds of the vote, it can only end up with either half or all the congressional seats.

Thus, another complication for any rule is that it will have to vary with the number of congressmen elected in a state. Just look at the largest 13 states with at least 10 congressmen each: nine of those states face a much greater vote gap than Texas. In Massachusetts, Democrats receive 20% more of the congressional seats than they receive of the congressional vote. In Ohio, the gap is 15% in Republicans' favor. Only three states other than Texas (California, Florida and New York) have at least 20 congressmen, and all three have larger percentage gaps than Texas.

Much of the political pressure in the Pennsylvania and Texas redistricting cases comes from the lack of political competitiveness. Only 33 out of 435 congressional seats are considered competitive this year. Ironically, it was a couple of politically sacred Supreme Court cases, the so-called "one-person one-vote" rulings from the 1960s, that helped create the current mess, making state legislative and—to a lesser extent—congressional elections much less competitive. Many states used to assign state legislators by county, just as U.S. senators are assigned by state, and there were wide discrepancies in how many constituents a state senator represented. But without the constraints of these political boundaries, politicians could draw almost any shape district they wanted so long as they all had the same number of people.

In the 1960s, Democrats wanted the one-person-one-vote rule because the rural districts with few people tended to be much more conservative than urban areas, and they were given disproportionate influence. Whatever its merits, few would have foreseen the current mess that these past rulings have helped create.

Other arguments regarding the number of majority-minority districts in Texas will also be considered by the Supreme Court, but those arguments are even weaker. After the switch to Republican control, for example, the number of Hispanic and African-American congressmen didn't decline.

Justice Kennedy was correct in the Pennsylvania case: it seems impossible for workable rules to define when gerrymandering goes too far. Hopefully, the Supreme Court will this time recognize the unintended consequences its actions can have.

Originally appeared March 1, 2006 in Wall Street Journal.

Partisan Bias in Newspapers?
A Study of Headlines Says Yes

with Kevin A. Hassett

Economists have been puzzled this year by the persistence with which perceptions about the economy have lagged the economic data. For the most recent 12-month period for which we have data, for example, the economy grew almost exactly as fast as it did during the best 12-month period during President Clinton's two terms. But the economic mood of the country has been much different.

It isn't just the economy that influences people's perceptions. In research we just released, we find that media coverage is also an important determinant. We found that newspaper headlines reporting economic news on unemployment, gross domestic product (GDP), retail sales, and durable goods tended to be much more frequently negative when a Republican was in the White House. And this was true even after accounting for the economic numbers on which the stories were based and how those numbers were changing over time.

We also found that positive headlines explained whether people thought that the economy was getting better more than the economic variables themselves. Newspapers are indeed important.

There have, of course, been numerous anecdotal claims of media bias. What has been lacking is a rigorous scientific study of media bias, and our new paper is an attempt to provide just that.

If we limit ourselves to news coverage of economic data, it is possible to get an objective measure of the news behind the stories. Our research team first collected a list of days that important economic news was released for most papers since 1991 and for four major papers and the Associated Press since 1985. We then used Lexis-Nexis, a computer database of news stories that contains information on 389 newspapers, to gather all of the 12,620 headlines that ran in America's newspapers covering economic news stories. We excluded follow-up and feature stories because we wanted to be able to link the headlines directly with the numbers on which they were based.

Headlines are relatively easy to classify since they say things are getting better, worse or mixed. For example, on January 31, the government reported that the real GDP had grown 4% in the fourth quarter of 2003. The *New York Times* covered this (appropriately) as good news, writing the headline, "Economy remained strong in 4th quarter, U.S. reports." At the same time, the *Chicago Tribune* wrote that "GDP growth disappoints; job worries linger." Headlines are so divergent, it's sometimes hard to believe they are referring to the same event.

Actual economic data explains much—but far from everything—about the headlines. We found that the incidence of positive coverage during Republican presidencies was fairly steady, but economic news under President Clinton received by far the most positive coverage. This partisan gap or bias (the difference in positive headlines between Republicans and Democrats for the same underlying economic news) consistently implied that Democrats got between 10 and 20% points more positive headlines.

We also examined individual newspapers. Among the top 10 papers, we found strong evidence that the Associated Press, the *Chicago Tribune*, the *New York Times*, and the *Washington Post* were much more likely to have positive headlines for Democrats even with the same economic news. The *New York Post* showed no statistically significant difference. The Los Angeles Times did not tend to treat Republicans and Democrats significantly differently.

Even including the *Los Angeles Times*, Ronald Reagan, a president who presided over one of the most vigorous economies in our history, still received 7% fewer positive news stories than Clinton after accounting for the different economic conditions.

What motivates newspapers and their copywriters to pick the headlines that they do is not a question we tried to answer. Whether these motivations are conscious or not, a partisan gap exists, and it helps explain one of this year's biggest economic puzzles. Unfortunately, the recent charges of political bias at CBS may only be a small part of the problem with the news.

Originally appeared October 6, 2004 in The Philadelphia Inquirer.